HISTORY WALKS IN NEW JERSEY

HISTORY WALKS IN NEW JERSEY

Exploring the Heritage of the Garden State

LUCY D. ROSENFELD

MARINA HARRISON

RIVERGATE BOOKS
An imprint of Rutgers University Press
New Brunswick, New Jersey, and London

Library of Congress Cataloging-in-Publication Data

Rosenfeld, Lucy D., 1939–

History walks in New Jersey : exploring the heritage of the Garden State / Lucy D. Rosenfeld and Marina Harrison.

p.   cm.

Includes index.

ISBN-13: 978–0-8135-3969-0 (pbk. : alk. paper)

1. Historic sites—New Jersey—Guidebooks.   2. New Jersey—History, Local—Guidebooks.   3. New Jersey—Tours.   4. Walking—New Jersey—Guidebooks.   I. Harrison, Marina, 1939–   II. Title.

F135.R67   2006

917.49'044—dc22

2006010753

A British Cataloging-in-Publication record for this book
is available from the British Library.

The publication of this volume has been made possible, in part, by a gift from Nicholas G. Rutgers IV and Nancy Hall Rutgers to support books about New Jersey.

Manufactured in the United States of America

CONTENTS

Introduction   ix

1 • PATERSON FALLS   I
  Magnificent Natural Beauty and Its Historic Uses

2 • WEEHAWKEN   6
  Memorials and Spectacular Views

3 • ELLIS ISLAND   10
  An Evocative Journey into America's Immigrant Experience

4 • FORT LEE   15
  America's First Movie Town

5 • UNDERCLIFF   22
  In Search of a Long-Gone Fishing Village on the Banks of the Hudson

6 • SKUNK HOLLOW   26
  A Nineteenth-Century African American Community

7 • RINGWOOD AND LONG POND   30
  An Ironworks Saga

8 • EDISON NATIONAL HISTORIC SITE   37
  Exploring an Extraordinary Legacy

9 • FELTVILLE   41
  A Forgotten Utopian Village in the Watchung Reservation

10 • HISTORIC SPEEDWELL   46
  A Village of Inventions

11 • PYRAMID MOUNTAIN   51
  A Leni-Lenape Legacy

12 • JOCKEY HOLLOW   55
  Woodland Trails and Soldiers' Huts

13• COOPER MILL AND THE BLACK RIVER   60
History amid Wooded Splendor

14• THE SUSSEX BRANCH RAIL TRAIL   64
Old Mines, Bridges, and Ruins

15• WATERLOO VILLAGE   68
A Walk through a Nineteenth-Century Canal Town

16• MILLBROOK VILLAGE   72
Exploring a Nineteenth-Century Ghost Town

17• HOPE   76
A Moravian Settlement

18• BELVIDERE   80
A Victorian Architectural Gem

19• CLINTON   86
A Riverside Mill Village and Quarry

20• THE PRALLSVILLE MILLS   91
*A Tiny Historic Gem and Walk along the
Delaware and Raritan Canal*

21• PRINCETON CEMETERY   95
Burial Site of Presidents and Other Notables

22• PRINCETON BATTLEFIELD STATE PARK   100
Scenes from the Revolutionary War

23• THE DELAWARE AND RARITAN CANAL   104
A Towpath and Rail Trail Loop from Kingston to Rocky Hill

24• WASHINGTON CROSSING STATE PARK   109
A Ferry Landing and Historical Center from the Revolutionary War

25• MONMOUTH BATTLEFIELD STATE PARK   113
Walking through Revolutionary War History

26• GEORGIAN COURT COLLEGE   117
The Robber Baron's Estate and the Glories of Excess and Elegance

27• TWIN LIGHTS OF NAVESINK   120
Exploring a Historic Lighthouse and Center of Invention

28 • ALLAIRE 124
A *Deserted Nineteenth-Century Village and Company Town*

29 • OCEAN GROVE 128
A *Victorian Camp Meeting Village on the Shore*

30 • CATTUS ISLAND AND BARNEGAT LIGHT 132
The Shore's Heritage of Pirates and Patriots

31 • DOUBLE TROUBLE AND WHITESBOG VILLAGES 136
Cranberry Towns in the Pinelands

32 • LAKEHURST 140
*The Naval Air Station, the History of Flight,
and the* Hindenburg *Disaster*

33 • HISTORIC WALNFORD 144
A *Mill Village Reflecting 250 Years of History*

34 • ROOSEVELT 148
A *New Deal Hideaway*

35 • BORDENTOWN 152
Architectural Pleasures from a Colonial Past to the Bonapartes

36 • BURLINGTON 158
New Jersey's Oldest Colonial Streetscape on the Delaware

37 • BURLINGTON AND ITS NEIGHBORS 163
Stops on the Underground Railroad

38 • ROEBLING 168
A *Turn-of-the-Century, One-of-a-Kind Factory Town*

39 • RANKOKUS INDIAN RESERVATION 172
An Introduction to Powhatan Renape Culture

40 • MOUNT HOLLY 175
A *Walking Tour through a Village of Colonial Beauty
and Quaker Roots*

41 • BATSTO 181
A *Bog Iron Forge Village in the Pine Barrens*

42 ◆ WHEATON VILLAGE   185
A Historic Small Town with Glassworks

43 ◆ RED BANK BATTLEFIELD   189
A Picturesque Riverside Historic Site and Walking Trail

44 ◆ FORT MOTT, PEA PATCH ISLAND,
AND THE FINN'S POINT NATIONAL CEMETERY   193
Coastal Ramparts, Towers, a Ferryboat Ride,
and Civil War Memories

45 ◆ GREENWICH   197
The Unspoiled Site of New Jersey's Own Revolutionary "Tea Party"

46 ◆ BRIDGETON   202
Exploring a Cumberland County City's Historic Legacy

47 ◆ EAST POINT LIGHTHOUSE TO MAURICETOWN   207
The Oyster Boat Route

48 ◆ CAPE MAY   210
From Colonial to Victorian Pleasures

Choosing an Outing   215
Index   219
Photo Credits   223

INTRODUCTION

New Jersey has had an unusually strong presence in many of the great movements and moments of the nation's history. From its early days as home to Native Americans, through its colonization by a great variety of peoples—the Swedes, English, Dutch, Moravians, Italians, Jews, Germans, and African Americans, to name just some of them—the state's history has reflected the larger American story. It played a vital role in the Revolutionary War, in the history of invention and transportation, in the Underground Railroad, in early mining and agricultural development, in seacoast adventure, in village life and the founding of utopian communities, and even in the beginnings of the movie industry.

We set out to find remaining evidence of this fascinating past—in both grand, well-recognized spots like scenic Revolutionary battlefields, and in smaller, more intimate locations such as hideaways for escaped slaves, evocative Civil War graveyards, and the wonderful ruins of mines in Jersey's mountains. Our criteria were simple: we wanted to combine historic interest with a true "outing"—a walk or bike ride that would convey an intrinsic sense of the past. This was not an easy task, as it turned out. So much of the state's history has been paved over, lost to time, or otherwise disregarded. Only in the last decades have steps been taken to save what's left—and our job, we felt, was to provide our readers with trips that they and their families or school classes can take to bring these many unusual and historic sites to a form of "living history."

While we have visited many wonderful historic houses and museums (and have included them in each description), we sought evidence of the historic past in unlikely spots as well. Where did the pirates of the Jersey shore hide to capture sea-borne cargo? Where did the shad fishermen of the Hudson live under the Palisade cliffs? Where did the Leni-Lenape celebrate the solstice? Where did so many presidents spend their summers? How did new inventions spark the lighthouses and industrial might of the nation? These and dozens of other questions led us to every corner of our state, and we hope our readers find the forty-eight locations we chose as historically and scenically fascinating as we did.

We include pertinent information on hours and openings, phones and Web sites, as well as directions. Though as of the date of publication this information was correct, we recommend you call or check Web sites to be sure nothing has changed.

As with all such complex projects, a number of people were invaluable in finding the answers to some difficult questions. We would like to acknowledge with grateful thanks the following: Norman Baron, Joan Geismar, Alice Calaprice, Claire Johnson, Pali Gall, Arlene Tice, Maria Esche, Professor Giles Wright, Teresa Wyman, and our always helpful husbands, Peter Rosenfeld and James Harrison.

It is our hope that our readers who take pleasure and interest in history will help to save similar sites near their homes, and will keep us informed of new and interesting discoveries.

HISTORY WALKS IN NEW JERSEY

1·
PATERSON
FALLS

Paterson Falls

Magnificent Natural Beauty and Its Historic Uses

❧ HOW TO GET THERE

From Route 80, take exit 57 to Route 19, Clifton. Take first exit at Valley Road. Turn right at top of ramp and follow signs.

❧ INFORMATION

Visitors are welcome to walk around the falls during daylight hours. The Great Falls Visitor Center, 65 McBride Avenue, is open 9 A.M. to 4 P.M. on weekdays, except holidays (and from May 1 to October 30 also on weekends, 1–4 P.M.). Since this spot can be somewhat isolated in places, we recommend visiting in broad daylight, when other tourists and walkers are around, or joining a guided tour. The falls are especially spectacular after a heavy rainfall. Telephone: 973-279-9587.

❧ Paterson, a city of mills and factories on the Passaic River, owes its surprisingly illustrious history to the Great Falls, one of the natural wonders of New Jersey and, in fact, of the nation. It was because of these majestic raging torrents, second in the East only to Niagara's in sheer volume, that Paterson was founded here, early in the country's history.

Alexander Hamilton, the first secretary of the Treasury, believed (unlike most other founding fathers) that the future of the country lay in an industrial—rather than an agrarian—economy. When he first saw the 77-foot high and 280-foot wide falls in 1778 (he and George Washington were standing next to each other on a rocky ledge opposite the falls), he was apparently even more struck by the implications of their might than by their dramatic beauty. Indeed, he envisioned them powering a great manufacturing center that would supply the needs of the country. Here was enough water power to turn mill wheels, and a river to transport manufactured goods to marketing centers.

With the assistance of the noted architect Pierre Charles L'Enfant, designer of Washington, D.C., Hamilton conceived a system of mills, water wheels, and elevated raceways that would carry water and produce energy from the Passaic River. (Never mind that L'Enfant's elaborate and grand design scheme proved to be too costly, and that the job had to be completed by Peter Colt.) The new manufacturing community was named after New Jersey's governor at the time, William Paterson, signer of the 1791 charter that established the Society for Establishing Useful Manufactures ("SUM") to subsidize the project. Unfortunately, Hamilton never lived to see his vision come to full fruition; he was killed in the famous duel with Aaron Burr several years before the War of 1812, when Paterson was finally enjoying a boom.

Though the city experienced the inevitable economic slumps, it grew steadily throughout much of the nineteenth century, first with its plentiful cotton mills, later with its important silk industry. By midcentury, it had become known internationally as "Silk City," and by 1900 it was the fifteenth largest city in the country. From this "cradle of American industry" also came the birth of the locomotive (by the 1880s Paterson was producing most of those made in the country), the Colt revolver, the first submarine, and even the airplane engine that Charles Lindbergh used in his famous transatlantic flight.

In the 1960s Paterson, like many other manufacturing cities in the Northeast, declined; even its majestic waterfall was substantially reduced through a curious bureaucratic decision to divert gallons of water daily. Fortunately, in 1976 the Great Falls district was designated a national historic landmark, which we hope is turning the city around once again. Today visitors can enjoy walking above the fully restored falls and wandering around the nearby historic district, where many old factories still remain. (Again, we recommend walking around during daylight hours and preferably not alone.)

As many times as we have visited and walked above the falls—for that is what you can do here—we are overwhelmed by their beauty. Leave your car at the parking lot opposite the Visitor Center, where you can pick up information on a self-guided walking tour or arrange for a guided tour. The walk we propose is easy and about 1.5 miles (slightly longer if you include visits to some of the mills), but you can create your own walk, too, by following whichever paths appeal to you, using the Great Falls as your compass. At river level, you might find a fisherman seated on a glacier rock in the midst of the swirling waters.

After leaving your car, walk to the overlook for a truly spectacular view of the falls, surrounded by massive basalt cliffs. Appropriately, you'll also find a monument to Alexander Hamilton nearby. From the overlook, walk back toward McBride and up the hill on Spruce Street toward the hydroelectric station, which lies below. Built between 1913 and 1914 and one of the oldest in the nation, it has been closed since 1969 but may eventually be reactivated. Follow a small path to Mary Ellen Kramer Park, named for the woman who fought to preserve this wonderful spot; the path leads to one footbridge, then another directly above the tumbling waters. The roar here can be deafening, especially after a heavy rainfall.

Turn left beyond the bridge, and go down some steps to another lookout point. Continue left, over the falls (you'll pass some nineteenth-century brick plants), turn left onto Wayne Avenue, over the river, left again onto McBride Avenue, and find a path on the other side of the street just before the intersection with Spruce Street, which leads to the Upper Raceway. The raceway, dating from the mid-1800s, drew water from the river and supplied it to the mills via an elaborate three-way system of spillways and canals. If you like early engineering and waterways—the first one here was built in 1792—this area will interest you.

Walk a few feet, turn left, and cross a bridge to the Middle Raceway, which will eventually lead to McBride Avenue again. Having made a full circle, at this point you can either return to the parking lot, or, if you're interested in seeing some of the old mills, turn back onto Spruce Street, where you'll find several of them, including the Rogers Locomotive Erecting Shop, built in 1835, which houses an exhibit on the history of industry in Paterson. You might then continue on to Barbour Street, for a flavor of olden times, cobblestones and all, and continue to explore the remains of Paterson's industrial grandeur.

❧ IN THE VICINITY

Lambert Castle Museum, 3 Valley Road, Paterson. This romantic site was the showplace home of Catholina Lambert, a silk magnate whose mills in Paterson were powered by the Great Falls. In the late 1890s this Englishman built his "castle" on Garrett Mountain to house not only himself and his family, but also his vast collection of art and antiquities. You can visit the castle, now operated by the Passaic County Historical Society, and see what is left of his collection.

The setting for this big stone structure is quite amazing: the castle is built on top of the mountain, appearing like a picturesque ruin, overlooking the urban scene below. The views are terrific! This romantic spot will also appeal to children, for it seems like a storybook castle. Telephone: 973-881-2761.

Paterson Museum, 2 Market Street. This fascinating museum details Paterson's role as the first planned industrial city in the nation. Its collection relates to the silk industry, mining, locomotives, and more. Telephone: 973-881-3874.

The Botto House/American Labor Museum, 83 Norwood Street, Haledon. This museum is housed in what was once the home of immigrant silk worker Maria Botto and her family. As a popular meeting place for fellow workers in nearby Paterson, it became the focal point for striking workers during the 1913 Paterson silk strike, which called for safe working conditions, an end to child labor, and an eight-hour work day. Now a National Historic Landmark, the museum exhibits chronicle the history of workers and the labor movement, as well as the immigrant experience in America. Telephone: 973-595-7953.

Garretson Farm County Historic Site, 402 River Road, Fair Lawn. Here you will be introduced to rural Dutch life in colonial times. Telephone: 201-646-2780.

The Radburn Association, 29–20 Fair Lawn Avenue, Fair Lawn. Radburn, a planned community dating from 1929, has inspired many similar communities worldwide. Designed to provide for the "complexities of modern life, while still providing the amenities of open space, community service, and economic viability," it was and remains a self-sufficient and self-contained entity governed by a fairly strict set of rules. The town is organized around clusters, with separate areas for pedestrians and automobiles; it includes 149 acres of interior parklands, as well as swimming pools, tennis courts, playgrounds and playing fields, and a large community center. If you're interested in urban planning, you'll enjoy a walk around this intriguing community.

Dey Mansion, 199 Totowa Road, Wayne. This house, one of George Washington's various headquarters, is now a museum featuring antiques. Telephone: 973-696-1776.

The Van Riper-Hopper Museum, 533 Berdan Avenue, Wayne, is a 1786 Dutch Colonial farmhouse. Telephone: 973-694-7192.

2·
WEEHAWKEN

Alexander Hamilton Bust in Weehawken

*Memorials
and Spectacular Views*

HOW TO GET THERE

Weehawken is a few miles south of the George Washington Bridge, just beyond Fort Lee, Cliffside Park, Guttenberg, and West New York.

INFORMATION

This walk is wonderful at any time of the year, and any time of day.

We don't know of another walk that so dramatically combines past and present. This is a truly extraordinary juxtaposition; here are the commemorative monuments that bring America's history very much to mind, contrasted with the scenic panorama of contemporary Manhattan stretched out in all its glory before you.

This long, straight expanse of New Jersey shoreline is high above the Hudson. Below, at the bottom of sheer rock face, are the bustling enterprises of ferry boats and commerce. The mighty Hudson travels swiftly along the shore, endlessly captivating the viewer with small boats, commuter ferries, great liners berthing in Manhattan, and tugs and barges making their ways up and down stream.

Across the river is Manhattan, laid out for your inspection like a three-dimensional stage set: you can recognize the great buildings centered around the Empire State Building. You can see the docks with their cruise ships, the traffic up and down the shore, the pale grays and tans and shiny steel of this grand metropolis with its unmatched skyline. Be sure to bring your camera. It looks glamorous from here and it seems to represent the glowing future.

And here, on the Jersey side, spaced within a mile or two are meaningful memorials to a past that helped make that city view possible in so many ways. Some of the memorials reflect a particular time and place; others commemorate American lives, from all over the nation, lost in wars. One represents a foreign hero who searched and fought for liberty. Anyone with a far-reaching interest in history will find this a thought-provoking walk, as will those of us who simply love great views.

This entire walk covers about 1.25 miles each way, though you can also do it in two shorter stretches, parking twice. In the middle is a section with no monuments, but there are always great views from a series of park walkways.

We begin at the northern end of the walk which cannot—by any kind of organization—be historically chronological. Park your car on Boulevard East at 60th Street, or just around the corner. On the waterside you'll find the most recent commemorative. Appropriately it is a graceful fountain with Lady Justice in the center and is a tribute to those lost to terrorist attacks in the great New York tragedy of September 11, 2001. Its setting, opposite the thriving city across the Hudson, is both poignant and fitting.

Continue south along the walkway to the next memorial. Here is Christopher Columbus in a sandstone relief. It has been only a little over five hundred years that he came upon the Americas.

About two-tenths of a mile farther along are two of the most compelling monuments: memorials to fallen soldiers in World War II and the Vietnam War. The first is a rather striking combination of a lethal-looking mounted gun, along with a nearby memorial. Words are not necessary here—there is merely a listing of familiar places: Anzio Beach, Pearl Harbor, and others. The Vietnam Memorial is more abstract. A white Aztec-style stepped pyramid is both tasteful and evocative. "Lest We Forget" are the words we remember.

Continue your walk to a monument at 54th street to José Martí, the patriot and leader of rebel troops against the Spanish in Cuba. This area of New Jersey is home to many Cuban Americans, and the memorial to Martí sits proudly among the other monuments to freedom.

The distance between the Martí statue and the next commemorative—also a war memorial—is some seven-tenths of a mile. Here you can divide your walk by returning to your car and driving along the scenic route, or continue, as we do, enjoying the view. But however you get there, be sure not to miss the last stops on this walk.

First is another scenic lookout with a war memorial and, a few hundred feet farther away, Hamilton Park, named for Alexander Hamilton. Keep walking south to the bust of Hamilton, which sits above a sheer cliff. It was partway down this rocky hill where a dueling ground was located, and it was here that Hamilton, the first secretary of the Treasury and a founding father of the country, was shot and killed by Aaron Burr, then vice president, in 1804. (Bicentennial reenactments have recently taken place here.) This spot—nowadays just above the busy Weehawken ferry to Manhattan—is where Hamilton and Burr also took a ferry across for their illegal and horribly ill-fated duel. If you stand in Hamilton Park and look at New York—the world's greatest financial capital—you can't help but think of Hamilton's prescient fiscal advice and policies.

3·
ELLIS ISLAND

Ellis Island

*An Evocative Journey into
America's Immigrant
Experience*

❀ HOW TO GET THERE

We take you there via the ferry from Liberty State Park in Jersey City. (There is also a ferry from Battery Park in Lower Manhattan.) From the New Jersey Turnpike, take exit 14B and follow signs to the park. Park your car next to the old railroad building at the north end of the park, where you can purchase tickets to the ferry.

❀ INFORMATION

The ferryboat ride from Liberty State Park to Ellis Island takes about ten minutes (the ferry then goes on to Liberty Island, which you can visit with the same ticket). There are many ferries daily, year-round (except Christmas Day), starting at 8:30 A.M. and leaving every forty-five minutes or so. For schedule and ticket information, call 201-435-9499, or go to www.nps.gov/stli on the Internet.

❀ It's hard to imagine a more evocative place to visit than Ellis Island, one of America's great landmarks. To appreciate this site you need not be among the 100 million Americans today whose ancestors came through these gates as immigrants in search of a better life. Just seeing the place that decided the fates of so many people over a span of more than fifty years, and bearing witness (of course very secondhand) to their incredible tenacity despite such hardships, cannot help but be a poignant experience for anyone with a feeling for American history and diversity. And, along with this fascinating glimpse into the past, you will also be rewarded with exhilarating views of the Statue of Liberty standing tall and proud nearby, surrounded by New York Harbor and the spectacular skyline. Here again, the old is juxtaposed with the new in an unforgettable way.

Ellis Island has a long history preceding its role as the gateway to America. Rich with waterbirds, it was called Gull Island by the local Indians, who enjoyed its bounty; it then became a hangout for pirates. Samuel Ellis, who owned the island in the late 1700s, developed it as a recreation spot; during the War of 1812 it became a fort, and later a munitions dump. In the 1890s a bill was passed to improve the island and turn it into an immigration depot (by then the immigrant population was rapidly escalating)—an unpractical decision, considering the fact that the surrounding waters were too shallow to dock boats and a ferry slip had to be dredged. On New Year's Day of 1892, a young Irish girl named Annie Moore became the first immigrant to enter this station.

Back in the heyday of the great immigration—between 1897 and 1938—the trip to Ellis Island was an ordeal. The millions (some 12 million, mostly Europeans) who descended en masse, sometimes at the rate of thousands a day, especially in the peak year of 1907, experienced grueling journeys that lasted weeks, sometimes months. These courageous souls, fleeing religious persecution, political strife, or unemployment, left everything familiar behind, hoping to start life anew.

Here at Ellis Island they would disembark by the shipload and prepare to take their first—and often humiliating—steps toward becoming Americans. Long lines of people would enter the building, where doctors and inspectors awaited them, checking them for contagious diseases and other illnesses, and marking them accordingly; they would then inch their way up the stairs to the daunting Registry Room to be asked countless questions. (It was here that new names were imposed on those whose surnames seemed unpronounceable.) Those who "passed" would go back downstairs, change money, and be on their way, while the unfortunate few who were detained faced the grim prospect of deportation. Dormitories were built to house hundreds of detainees, sometimes as many as three hundred people in triple-tiered bunks in one room. By 1924 its role was diminished and in 1954 it was declared "surplus property." Restoration of the deteriorating buildings was begun years later, in the 1980s. The spankingly refurbished Ellis Island Immigration Museum—its turrets and tiles resplendent once again—opened its doors on September 10, 1990; since then, Ellis Island has again seen millions of "visitors" reach its shores—some 2 million a year.

When planning your trip to Ellis Island you should decide first whether you might also wish to visit Liberty Island on the same trip (your tickets are valid for both stops), since doing both would obviously necessitate catching an earlier ferry. You'll find the ferryboat ride truly spectacular and may even wish it lasted longer. As you approach, Lady Liberty comes into full view, her gleaming torch an inspiration to millions of people. And just before her lies Ellis Island's distinctive brick and limestone main building with its four turrets. Surrounding the building is a little park shaded with trees, the impressive Wall of Honor (more about that later), as well as several other buildings once used as hospitals and dormitories for which further restorations are planned.

The ferry pulls up just feet from the entrance to the main building. Inside this cavernous structure are three floors of exhibits tracing Ellis Island's history. You can take your own, self-guided tour (audio tours and several different brochures are available) or arrange for a guided tour. There is something for everyone in this efficiently run premier tourist site, which attracts so many visitors from all over. On the ground floor, next to the information desk, you are greeted with a fascinating collection of sundry trunks, suitcases, baskets, and makeshift whatnots used by the immigrants to transport their belongings. Behind this exhibit are others relating to the immigrant experience, including poignant photographs of the life of immigrants. Should you wish to trace your ancestry, see the American Family Immigration History Center, or ask at the Information Center. On this floor, too, are several theaters (pertinent films are routinely shown).

Walk up the stairs to the imposing Great Hall, the Registry Room with its elegant arched windows and newly minted 56-foot-high barrel-vaulted ceiling. This remarkable ceiling was rebuilt in 1917 by a Spanish immigrant named Rafael Guastavino, who developed a self-supporting system of interlocking terra-cotta tiles. He did such a careful job and secured the tiles so well that only 17 of the 28,832 had to be replaced during the restoration. In the hall you'll also find tall wooden desks, where immigrants were questioned and registered. On both ends of the hall are additional exhibition spaces. The third floor houses more exhibits, including the "Dormitory Room," as well as a library, reading room, and conference room.

There is much to see within the museum (the museum brochure recommends a minimum of three hours to do it justice), and much outside, too. First of all, the vistas: before you are the skylines of Manhattan, Brooklyn, and nearby Jersey City, their buildings and bridges shining brightly, and of course the Statue of Liberty. Take a moment to enjoy the captivating comings and goings on the river, for here, in New York Harbor, you'll see a lot of action. Then wander through the green park to the "Wall of Honor," an impressive circular steel wall bearing the names of 600,000 immigrants who came to America from the 1830s until it closed. We were astonished at the columns of names that seemed to go on forever.

The other buildings on Ellis Island (once dormitories, hospitals, etc.) are not open to the public, as they are mostly in a state of decay. The WPA-era ferry building, which now looks so forlorn, is apparently going to be renovated in the near future, and we hope the others will be as well. Meanwhile, there is more than enough to see on Ellis Island, and a visit here is a memorable experience for all.

✿ IN THE VICINITY

Upon your return by ferry to Liberty State Park, you might wish to see what this lovely park offers—if you still have time and energy. Having just immersed yourself in the immigrant experience you might be interested in taking a quick look at the huge, echoing train station (where you bought the tickets for the ferry), an 1889 red brick edifice: it was here that some 8 million immigrants boarded trains that took them to their new destinations. Along the shoreline and beyond are lovely, scenic pathways, where it is a real treat to walk on a bright, sunny day and take in more of the wondrous views surrounding you. Within the 88-acre park (dedicated in 1976 as New Jersey's gift to the nation) are also various exhibition areas and the impressive Liberty Science Center, a great place to take children. The park is open daily, dawn to dusk. There are no fees except for parking and taking the ferry.

4·
FORT LEE

The Palisades at Fort Lee

America's First Movie Town

❧ HOW TO GET THERE

Fort Lee is the last town in New Jersey before crossing the George Washington Bridge into Manhattan. Take the last exit before the bridge from any of the major New Jersey highways (Routes 80, 95, 46, or the Palisades Parkway) onto Main Street/Fort Lee.

To see where movie cliff shots were taken, go to Alison Park or the Long Path, starting at the George Washington Bridge.

Alison Park (Englewood Cliffs)

From Palisades Parkway, take exit 1 to Hudson Terrace (south); take first left off Hudson Terrace, follow signs to Alison Park, and walk toward the river. Long Path entrance: Continue south on Hudson Terrace and park on the street, just north of the George Washington Bridge, on the northbound side of the road where there are parking meters. Find a metal staircase going up for access to the Long Path. At the top of the steps turn right toward the river and follow a narrow gravel path that leads to lookouts over the Palisades cliffs.

Fort Lee Historic Park

Continue south on Hudson Terrace, go under the bridge, and make a left at the park entrance, about one block south of the bridge.

Fort Lee Historic Society and Museum

In Fort Lee take Main Street east toward the river, and turn right two blocks past the Lemoine Avenue intersection. The museum is at the Judge Moore House, a small stone building off Parker Street (though its official address is 1588 Palisades Avenue).

Rambo's Hotel

Once the famed Rambo's Hotel, this now private house (which can be seen from the outside only), is located at 2423 First Street in Fort Lee. Take Main Street to Lemoine Avenue; go north, past the GW Bridge, and turn left at Myrtle Street. You'll find this visibly traditional house (surrounded by all new houses) directly across the street from the playing field to School #3.

❧ INFORMATION

You can walk around Alison Park or on the Long Path, free of charge, during daylight hours at any time of year, though paths may be icy and slippery in winter. (In the case of the Long Path, we recommend going with another person, as there are some isolated spots.)

Fort Lee Historic Park is open year-round, Wednesday–Sunday, from 10 A.M. to 4:30 P.M. Parking fee in season. Telephone: 201-461-3956. Web site: www. njpalisades.org.

Fort Lee Historic Society and Museum is open on Saturdays and Sundays, noon–4, and during the week by special appointment only. Telephone: 201-592-3580.

In addition, the Fort Lee Film Commission sponsors occasional tours of the old "film town," as well as showings of old films shot in Fort Lee. For information, go to their Web site (www.fortleefilm.org) or contact the Historic Society.

Unless you're quite a cinema buff and know something about the history of the American movie industry, you might well be surprised to learn that Fort Lee was the first "Hollywood." Yes, Fort Lee, the busy and often congested town surrounding the George Washington Bridge, which today appears as a motley combination of glittering high-rises and constantly new constructions that are randomly mixed in with modest buildings of another era. But, aside from its commercial aspects, Fort Lee enjoys a magnificent natural setting, one that remains forever unchanged, high above the dramatic Palisades cliffs and the Hudson River. Unquestionably this remarkable setting has played a key role in determining the town's unusual story.

The Fort Lee area became an important strategic site at the time of the American Revolution. Here a fort was built in 1776, on a spot overlooking the Palisades. (For more details, see the Fort Lee Historic Park, described below.) Named after General Charles Lee, the second-in-command who had assisted George Washington in the defense of New York City and the Hudson River, the fort had to be abandoned very suddenly in the face of a major British onslaught. For the Americans this abrupt retreat was understandably one of the darkest moments of the war, one that prompted these often quoted words from Thomas Paine (who had been here with Washington's army): "These are the times that try men's souls."

Flash forward to Fort Lee around 1907, when it was first "discovered" by the early moviemakers. Overnight, this sleepy village of dirt roads, which had just been incorporated in 1904, was transformed into America's first movie capital, remaining active in the business until the 1920s, while Hollywood was still in its infancy. But why was this relatively obscure little place chosen in the first place?

As they say, "Location, location, location!" The story begins in the first decade of the twentieth century, when film companies were starting to look for new shooting locations. Thomas Edison, who in addition to his many other creative activities was a film pioneer (he patented a machine called the Kinetoscope and also built the first movie studio in the world), was largely instrumental in bringing the fledgling movie industry to the area in the first place. Though New York City was the favored location for outdoor shoots, it obviously lacked the scenic country vistas for filming westerns, which were becoming more and more popular. Enter New Jersey's Fort Lee: not only were its dramatic sheer cliffs perfect for filming "wild west" scenes, but it was also surrounded with farms, woods, fields, and mountains, offering a great variety of scenery. In addition, Fort Lee (and such neighboring towns as Coytesville and Edgewater), was sparsely populated and uncongested; though fairly rustic, it did already have a number of restaurants and hotels (especially Rambo's Hotel, which looked just like a western saloon), a convenience for movie crews; with its old-fashioned houses and dirt roads, it already looked like an old western town; and being directly across the river from Manhattan, it was certainly much closer than the movie locales in the Catskills and Long Island.

The first of many films that would use the Palisades for exterior scenes was Edison's *Rescued from an Eagle's Nest* (1907), featuring noted director D. W. Griffith in his first acting role. As the word spread, a flood of film companies suddenly appeared—Champion, Paragon, Universal, World-Peerless, Willat, Fox, Goldwyn, Seznick, as well as the French companies Eclair, Pathé, and Solax. They built studios in Fort Lee and environs and began making one movie after another—so many, in fact, that it was not uncommon for several companies to be shooting at the same time. The town was now bustling with activity, with make-believe cowboys, Indians, knights, royal princesses, or sailors walking down Lemoine Avenue or Main Street along with their entourage. A good third of the locals were actually employed by the studios—in building sets, renting equipment, or working as extras. Apparently even children were hired (and paid $1 apiece) to appear in the films.

By far the favorite local "hangout" was Rambo's, a saloonlike hostelry where actors and production staff would congregate under a grape arbor to enjoy a meal with a good dose of daily gossip, or use the upstairs as makeshift dressing rooms to clean up after a day's shooting. Outsiders would gather here, too, hoping for a part in a film. Rambo's was also a premier film location, used in many films for its "western" look. (The pictur-esque old building has since been renovated and is now a private home sur-rounded by brand new houses, as described below.)

And who were the actors who worked here? Along with the hundreds whose names might not be familiar to us today were Rudolph Valentino, Norma Shearer, Mary Astor, Douglas Fairbanks, Lillian Gish, Mary Pick-ford (who made at least a dozen films here), Mack Sennett, Fatty Arbuckle, Ronald Coleman, Tallulah Bankhead, and the Barrymores, all of whom later became Hollywood stars. Even such nonactors as the magician Houdini and baseball player Babe Ruth appeared in local films. Notable directors included D. W. Griffith (he made some eighty films here), Mack Sennett, and Alice Guy Blaché, the first woman director in film history and chief executive of the Solax Studio.

And the films themselves? Among the many, a few like *The Raven, The Hungry Heart, House of Hate,* and the especially memorable *The Perils of Pauline* stand out. The latter two, starring the amazing Pearl White, were filmed atop the cliffs and involved daredevil stunts and thrills for everyone (on one occasion the actress found herself on a drifting balloon whose rocky anchor had loosened, eventually landing near Philadelphia). The term "cliffhanger" was actually coined from *The Perils of Pauline,* a serial film whose title character was always getting into all sorts of precarious situations, such as dangling over the cliffs, holding onto a little tree for dear life.

The era of intense moviemaking in Fort Lee ended by the early 1920s, as one studio after another closed, though some survived for years as film laboratories and storage vaults. But why did the studios leave Fort Lee for California? For one thing, the weather in Hollywood was certainly warmer and more predictable. Also, Fort Lee's transportation system was problematic: to reach the town from New York, one had to take a ferry, then a trolley up to the cliffs, all of which took too much time. Major labor disputes and unrest erupted here after the war as well, causing seri-ous difficulties (in California labor unions were not yet as organized). Fiinally, fires and explosions in some Fort Lee studios and laboratories destroyed everything.

Today there are few physical traces left of the film industry in Fort Lee. Most of the buildings that housed studios no longer exist (many were quite flimsy to begin with), having been lost to fire or neglect; the same is true of most of the films made during those magical years, as the majority survive only in the form of still photographs. However, Fort Lee's cinema heritage continues, largely through the efforts of museums, archives, libraries, and private collections and the recently created Fort Lee Film Commission; a few feature films are still shot here each year. The town of Fort Lee has begun to put up markers next to some relevant movie sites for easy identification; and you can still visit some of the sites that were part of Fort Lee's movie history.

The most important of these sites are the majestic Palisades themselves, of course. Though you can view them from different places (including the George Washington Bridge), we propose two walks that will give you good perspectives on the "cliffhanger" locations.

First is Alison Park, a very pretty little park situated right on the Palisades in Englewood Cliffs, the next town to the north of Fort Lee. Here are pathways along woods and grassy areas that lead to a walkway overlooking the Hudson, where you can spot rocky ledges; they could well be the very ones that appeared in such films as *The Perils of Pauline*. As you look down over those sheer drops, you can see what kept the audiences in such suspense!

The other walk we recommend is the "Long Path." Because of its length (about 248 miles from the GW Bridge all the way to Albany) we suggest you concentrate on just a small segment in the southernmost section. Here, in a very pretty and rustic woodsy area (without amenities), you can enjoy wonderful views of the Palisades and the river, as well as the larger-than-life bridge before you. The narrow gravel and dirt paths tend to be unattended, so be sure not to walk alone; and, again, be careful not to venture off the walkways as you gaze at the cliffs and surrounding vistas.

Before trying to locate further remnants of Fort Lee's movie past, we recommend a visit to the Fort Lee Historic Society and Museum (see above for hours and information). This tiny museum, housed in a 1920s stone building known as the Judge Moore House, is filled with fascinating photos, articles, movies, and artifacts documenting Fort Lee's history, including its movie era. When we were there, the enthusiastic and knowledgeable curator offered practical information (how to locate various sites, etc.) and also regaled us with local movie lore and legend.

The famed Rambo's Hotel is another site you won't want to miss. Though now a private home, you can see it from the outside as you drive or walk past it. And, despite some remodeling, it is still easily recognizable as the only vintage building on a street of all brand new houses; note its front porch posts, which appear just as they did in vintage photographs.

For a taste of Fort Lee's much earlier years—its role during the Revolutionary War—visit the Fort Lee Historic Park. Set on 33 acres atop the Palisades, the park has breathtaking views of the river, the bridge with its imposing architecture, and the glamorous cityscape beyond. As you stand on the cliffs, you can see why George Washington (who was a trained surveyor) picked this high spot to defend the Hudson; from here you can see everything that happens on the river. The fortification on this site was complemented by Fort Washington, a twin fort on the opposite side of the Hudson. Unfortunately, neither fort could stop the British under Cornwallis, whose army of six thousand strong landed just six miles north of here, marched south, and would have overwhelmed the Americans had they not retreated.

The park has outdoor displays—reconstructed gun batteries and a replica of a soldier's hut (about three hundred of these housed Washington's troops in the winter of 1776 before their forced retreat); you'll also find inviting paths leading to spectacular lookouts and a picnic area. Through its "living history" program, the park sponsors activities relating to life in the eighteenth century, such as casting musket balls or gathering and chopping firewood to make a stew following traditional recipes. Schoolchildren are frequent visitors and sometime participants. The Visitor Center, one of the most comprehensive in all of New Jersey, includes exhibits relating to the Revolutionary War era—military uniforms, weapons, and campaigns.

5·
UNDERCLIFF

Undercliff on the Hudson

In Search of a
Long-Gone Fishing Village
on the Banks of the Hudson

❀ HOW TO GET THERE

From the George Washington Bridge take the Palisades Parkway north to exit 1. Bear left after the exit ramp and go down the steep (but wide) road. Follow the signs to the Englewood Boat Basin, where you can park your car, preferably at the northern end of the huge parking lot, past playgrounds, picnic areas, and fishing docks. Walk north (with the river on your right) to find the footpath along the water. Undercliff was located in this area.

❀ INFORMATION

The footpath, known as the Shore Path, extends all the way to the Alpine Boat Basin, more than 5 miles. Though the trail is never crowded, we recommend you go off-season, rather than in summer when the parking lot can be crowded. The trail is mostly flat and easy, except for a few stone stairs near the Alpine Boat Basin. Parking fee between Memorial Day and Labor Day only. If you decide to walk all the way to the Alpine Boat Basin, you might arrange to be met there by car rather than retracing your steps.

❀ The towering, majestic cliffs of the Palisades are among the great natural wonders of the region. Situated on the west bank of the Hudson River, most dramatically visible as you cross the George Washington Bridge into New Jersey, they extend north for about 40 miles. Beneath these cliffs once stood a small but very active village of fishermen. "Undercliff," as it was aptly called, was a 10-mile-long settlement located on the narrow strip between the foot of the cliffs, below Englewood and Alpine, and the river. A bustling community of eight hundred people, for more than one hundred years it was home to shad fishermen, as well as boat builders, raftsmen, and, later on, quarrymen. Given the fact that it included many structures—houses, a school, church, tavern, graveyard—it's somewhat surprising that hardly a trace of it remains except for a few old gravestones now virtually hidden by dense foliage. But if you enjoy searching for clues—while taking an especially scenic walk along the river—we invite you to follow the Shore Path below the Palisades in the footprints of this lost village.

Though the trail is at least 10 miles long (it goes all the way to the New York State line), we recommend the section between the Englewood Boat Basin and the Alpine Boat Basin (or whatever part you can manage), the area where Undercliff once existed. The Shore Path is close to the river at all times and features a wonderful variety of terrain along the shore, including a long, slender waterfall and the ruins of a large 1930s bathing pavilion. In addition to its spectacular views of the overhead cliffs and the river, the path offers peace and quiet; you will not meet more than a walker or two, and (though you are in fact so close to New York City) you might hear only the sound of the wind blowing through the trees, the gently lapping water, or an occasional motorboat making its way up or down the river.

The Hudson River was not always as quiet as it is today; in the eighteenth and nineteenth centuries it teemed with life and activity. The water was clear and unpolluted, and fishing plentiful; and schooners and sloops navigated up and down and across the river, carrying rocks and bricks and farm produce to New York City markets. During Undercliff's early days—in the late 1700s—fishing was at the very center of its life. The first settlers, many of Dutch descent, realized they could make a decent living in the shad fishing industry (Hudson River shad was in great demand throughout the country). These fishermen enjoyed enormous catches in their nets each spring, when the shad were running. Large racks for drying shad nets along the shoreline were part of the local scene. The families lived comfortably but modestly along the shore in small white cottages with picket fences—in sharp contrast to the grand castlelike mansions that began to sprout on top of the cliffs in the 1850s (not to mention the enormous and luxurious resort hotel overlooking the Palisades, the Palisades Mountain House, which added to the area's prosperity by attracting people from all over the country).

Eventually, other groups settled in Undercliff—at first, boatbuilders and the raftsmen who transported building stones and logs down the river to the city. Then came the quarrymen. To satisfy the city's increasing demand for rock to pave city blocks, the infamous demolition of the Palisades began to take place—a lucrative operation for the residents of Underhill. The noise of black powder blast that sent the trap-rock crashing down to the river must have been deafening, and the transporting of so many tons of rock arduous. As John Allison, a member of a notable old Englewood family and an artist and chronicler, later described it, "Trig and sturdy must have been the sloops and other craft which slid down the ways of the Undercliff boatbuilders. Staunch indeed to stand the wear of the treacherous cargo of which New York City was gradually spreading itself."

By the 1870s the cliffs were seriously threatened, and a movement to "save the Palisades" began to take hold; at the same time, the railroad appeared in the region, undercutting the use of the Hudson for commerce. It was the beginning of the end for Undercliff, whose livelihood had depended on quarrying and river transportation. By the time the Palisades Parkway Commission took over in 1900 and bought out estates and quarries, the Underwood settlement had virtually died. Besides the cemetery, only a handful of houses remained—by 1911 only eight or ten, mostly occupied by elderly widows—and those eventually faded away.

Even if you never find any sign of Underhill (including those gravestones!), you will enjoy the wondrous beauty of this walk. After parking your car at the Englewood Boat Basin (once an extension of the Undercliff village), proceed north to find the shore path. The first "ruin" you will come to has nothing to do with Underhill itself, as it was built in the 1930s as a bathhouse for "Bloomer's Beach" (even though it's hard to imagine the Hudson River as a popular swimming area). Now roofless, it is an intriguing stone structure with imposing steps. As you continue walking, you'll note that the path's surface—at first sandy—becomes progressively grassy, then somewhat rocky, then woodsy. It was along here and beyond that Underhill's inhabitants lived. The cemetery—or whatever is left of it—is located about one mile north from the boat basin amid a meadow; hidden by overgrown vegetation and rocks from the cliffs, it's a real challenge to find.

The winding path, always shaded and pleasant, skirts the river, at times so close you can touch the water. You walk past small beaches and docks (from where the boats carrying their heavy loads sailed) and rocky lookout points. Trees grow down to the riverbank, and honeysuckle and grapevines, tall grasses, and shrubs of wild berries adorn the way. After some 3 miles or so you come to the picturesque Greenbrook Falls, amid a deeply wooded setting. The path then becomes steeper, with occasional stone steps up and down; this is a particularly scenic area, with a wide variety of vegetation and terrain. After another mile or so (a little over 5 miles from the Englewood boat basin), you arrive at the Alpine Boat Basin, where there are more fishing docks, no doubt once used by the fishermen of Underhill. From here you can either retrace your steps (for an additional 5-mile trek), or—if you were very clever and planned ahead—meet a car at the parking area of the boat basin to take you back.

6·
SKUNK HOLLOW

Skunk Hollow

A Nineteenth-Century
African American Community

❀ HOW TO GET THERE

The site of Skunk Hollow is located within the Palisades Interstate Park, in the northeast corner of Bergen County, less than one mile from the New York State line. It can be accessed from the State Line Lookout, between exits 2 and 3 from the Palisades Interstate Parkway.

❀ INFORMATION

Park grounds and trails are open daylight hours, year-round. The Lookout Inn (bookshop with park maps) is also open daily year-round. Telephone for hours, which vary according to season: 201-750-0465. For information on the park call 201-768-1360 during office hours, Monday–Friday, 8:30 A.M. to 4:30 P.M.

❀ This walk takes you to the northeast corner of Bergen County where Route 9W and the Palisades Parkway meet, a hilly area of about 100 acres known by locals as "the mountain," with deep woods, rocky terrain, and extraordinary views over the Hudson River. On this site, now endowed with a variety of trails for walkers, hikers, and cross-country skiers, there once existed a vibrant community of former slaves. "Skunk Hollow" (apparently so called because of the lush stands of skunk cabbage found there in springtime) was first settled in 1806 and thrived for about one hundred years. Few traces of the community remain, and even those are difficult to find or identify, lying mostly buried in the dense foliage; but walking along inviting wooded paths searching for the random stone foundations, cellar holes, and other pieces of evidence is a fascinating experience if you're interested in history or archaeology—regardless of what you might find (or not)!

Skunk Hollow was a one-of-a-kind rural community in New Jersey, composed of freed African Americans at a time when slavery was still very much an issue in the state. Why did this group of people come here in the first place? In the early nineteenth century, unlike the present, the area was not considered a desirable place to settle. The terrain was obviously as rocky as it is today, making it unsuitable for large-scale farming; it was also desolate then (most trees had been cut down for firewood) and subject to border disputes between the two states. It's not surprising that land here was relatively inexpensive.

The first settler was Jack Earnest. Having bought his freedom from a Bergen County farmer for $100, he purchased 5 acres atop the Palisades for

$87.50 in 1806. He and his wife were able to grow a few crops for their own use, but supported themselves as day laborers, as did most Skunk Hollow settlers. Soon they were joined by other freed slaves—James Oliver and Benjamin Charlton are two of these early names—and the community was launched.

Between the 1870s and 1880s, Skunk Hollow's population peaked at about seventy-five people, including twelve or thirteen active households, some twenty structures, and its own Methodist Episcopal church, the center of life in the hamlet. The community's binding force was no doubt its resident minister, William Thompson, affectionately called "Uncle Billy," who lived here from 1856 (when Earnest, at his deathbed, sold him his property) until his own death in 1886. During his three decades as spiritual leader, he saw Skunk Hollow evolve from a segregated enclave to a cohesive village. The men worked mostly as field laborers on nearby farms, while the women stayed at home and tended to their families. Some inhabitants may also have been involved in shoemaking on the side, as large amounts of leather were discovered on the site. It seems, in any case, that everyone lived contentedly. According to Dr. Joan Geismar, a prime authority on Skunk Hollow (who has collected more than 12,000 pieces of ceramics, glass shards, locks, and other relics from the site), "from the scanty tax records available, [we know that] the people of Skunk Hollow, as poor as they were, were wealthier than other free blacks."

After Thompson's death, Skunk Hollow began to fall apart as a community, eventually fading out by 1906. Meanwhile, "Turkey Ridge," an extension of it on the New York side of "the mountain," continued to function. Consisting of black, white, and intermarried families (and bearing such names as Oliver, Sisco, and Obleni), Turkey Ridge lived on until the 1950s, when the Palisades Interstate Parkway was built along here, disrupting existing communities.

If you would like to read further about Skunk Hollow before taking your walk, we recommend Dr. Geismar's book, based on her doctoral dissertation, *The Archaeology of Social Disintegration in Skunk Hollow,* which is highly informative and comprehensive. We also suggest you plan to explore the area in late fall or early spring, when the leaves are off the trees, making it easier to spot remnants of old stone walls and cellar holes. (It's also a time when you are not likely to meet up with any snakes, often found lurking around the rocks in summer.) Also: be sure to stay on the trails and be careful of poison ivy, which runs rampant—don't handle any vines, even when the leaves are off.

After you've parked your car at the lookout, walk north on "Old 9W," a paved roadway (closed to traffic) that runs parallel to the Hudson. Along the way don't miss the scenic lookouts over the river. Follow the signs for the C and D trails (the trails are joined in places). The "D" trail eventually winds back to the paved roadway, where you can retrace your steps back to your car.

You'll be walking up and down hills through dense woodlands, so wear stout shoes. If you're lucky you might find signs of the stone walls that formed boundaries between individual properties, and possibly even bits of pottery and old bottles here and there. You might also note depressions that were once cellars and foundations for houses. The site of the church is on a strip of land between the Palisades Parkway and Route 9W, and we don't recommend crossing either of those busy highways on foot to search for it. But don't be discouraged if you don't find the evidence you're looking for. Use your imagination as you walk in these beautiful woods, and you might well envision Skunk Hollow and the life of its inhabitants.

⚜ IN THE VICINITY

Wortendyke Barn, 13 Pascack Road, Park Ridge, is one of the last existing examples of a Colonial Dutch barn. It houses a small museum, including horse-drawn vehicles and antique tools. Telephone: 201-930-0124.

7·
RINGWOOD
AND LONG POND

Long Pond ruins

An Ironworks Saga

❧ HOW TO GET THERE

Ringwood Manor (Ringwood State Park)

The park and manor are located on Sloatsburg Road in Ringwood. From the New York Thruway, take Route 17 north. Follow signs toward Ringwood, about 8 miles from the intersection. Look for the entrance on your right.

Long Pond Ironworks Historic District

Located on Route 511, 2 miles east of Greenwood Lake, in the hamlet of Hewitt. From Route I-287 southbound (from NY Thruway) take exit 57 (Skyline Drive); follow Skyline Drive to its end. At intersection with Route 511 (Greenwood Lake Turnpike) turn right (onto 511); go about 6–7 miles (around Wanaque Reservoir and Monksville Reservoir dam). After Monksville Reservoir causeway you'll find the Long Pond Ironworks Visitor Center on your right.

From Long Pond to Ringwood

Left on Route 511 and right onto Sloatsburg Road until you come to Ringwood State Park (on your left).

❧ INFORMATION

Ringwood State Park is open year-round from 8 A.M. to 8 P.M. Tours of the manor are offered Wednesday through Sunday on the hour, between 10 A.M. and 3 P.M., but call first to confirm. Telephone: 973-962-7031. Web site: www.ringwoodmanor.com.

Long Pond Ironworks Historic District: Open year-round, 8 A.M. to 8 P.M. Museum is open on weekends, April through November, 11 A.M.–4 P.M. Tours of the site are offered at 10 A.M., noon, and 2 P.M. on the second weekend of every month, but call first to confirm. Telephone (information line): 973-657-1688; Web site: www.longpondironworks.org.

❧ Set within the Wanaque River Valley, amid the hilly and rural terrain of the Ramapo Mountains (near the New York State border) are two exceptional and very different sites. One, Ringwood Manor, is an elegant and unusual country manor within a large park; the other, Long Pond Ironworks Historic District, is an archeological site featuring the remains of a historic ironworks community.

The common theme of these two contrasting places is the iron industry of the Highlands region, which was so crucial to the state's and country's history. Located in an area that offered the perfect combination of natural resources for making iron, these mines were important in peacetime as well as wartime, from the Revolution through World War I. Because the two sites are only a few miles apart from each other and have had a long association—Ringwood Manor was home to Long Pond's iron-masters from the Revolutionary War until the 1880s—you might find it interesting to visit them both on the same day. A road built in the eigh-teenth century known today as the Hasenclever Iron Trail (named after Peter Hasenclever, one of the first ironmasters and developers in the area) connects the two sites. (It once linked the iron furnaces of both.) If you are an energetic hiker and can spare the extra time, consider this historic 5.73-mile trail as an alternative to driving from one place to the next. Make sure to pick up a detailed brochure of the trail, available at the Long Pond Vis-itor Center.

The Ringwood region was developed back in colonial times for its rich supply of iron ore. Though the earliest European settlers arrived in the 1600s, it wasn't until 1739 that the first iron forge was built, followed by more elaborate forges and furnaces. In midcentury the enterprising Hasenclever created the American Iron Company. Bringing with him an army of workmen from Ireland and Germany, he built cabins, storehouses, a gristmill and sawmill, and dams for water power—and saw great pros-perity (until, disgraced for spending too much money, he returned to Europe, bankrupt). Robert Erskine, a brilliant Scottish engineer, then managed the company. During the Revolutionary War he sided with the Americans and joined George Washington's staff as an army geographer. Erskine prepared at least three hundred invaluable maps for the Continen-tal Army, many of which are on display today in various museums. He is buried in a simple grave at Ringwood.

The ironworks prospered during much of the nineteenth century. The forges furnished munitions for the War of 1812 and the Civil War. The iron made here was considered particularly suited for gun manufacture. At midcentury the great entrepreneur and inventor, Peter Cooper, purchased the mines as well as the Ringwood manor house, which he turned into a much grander place to suit his lifestyle, and surrounding acres. His son-in-law, Abram S. Hewitt, a prominent industrialist and politician who even-tually became mayor of New York, succeeded him as ironmaster and made Ringwood Manor his summer home.

There are many tales concerning this bit of Americana. (You can read more about the ironmasters and their lives in books and brochures available at both visitor centers.) By the end of the nineteenth century it became more efficient to produce iron from the Great Lakes and Pennsylvania; the ironworks in this region thus began to suffer, though some remained active through World War I. Finally, both Ringwood and Long Pond were donated to the state, turned into parkland, and designated as National Historic Landmarks.

You can visit the two sites in whichever order you choose, but for the sake of chronology, we'll begin here with Long Pond. When you reach the tiny hamlet of Old Hewitt, look for the Visitor Center/Museum (formerly the Olde Country Store) right by the side of Route 511. It lies directly across the street from the Hewitt Methodist Church, a picturesque structure dating from 1895. Here you can pick up the walking guide to the 175-acre Long Pond Ironworks Historic District, which includes a recommended one-mile loop with stops along the way. (Since several of the structures shown on their map are now gone—or have yet to be unearthed—you will have to use your imagination.) You'll follow a rustic trail, not always clearly marked, as you wind your way through somewhat rugged, hilly, woodsy terrain dotted with ruins still being excavated and restored. This is a fascinating archeological site, where you can wander freely about the grounds, discovering crumbling foundations of cold cellars and the remains of old furnaces and dilapidated stores, houses, and dormitories that once housed workers. And you are not likely to meet more than a handful of visitors along the way—if any at all.

In its heyday, Long Pond included the workers' village as well as the ironworks themselves—furnaces, waterwheel, and forges, strategically placed near the Wanaque River. Note that some of the houses now found in the village were brought in from other locations, after the Monksville Reservoir was flooded in the 1980s. An early twentieth century sawmill and ice house were added after the iron industry gave way to other enterprises, such as ice harvesting, lumbering, and farming.

From the Visitor Center you can follow a wood-chip path that leads you to the first group of historic houses, including two old farmhouses. Continue to the large brookside Stone Double House, perhaps the oldest in the village, dating from 1760; if you look to your left you can see the ruins of an ice-pond dam. Take the wooden bridge across the river to the central section of the village. If you pursue the trail on your left you'll see a variety of ruins and foundations; straight ahead at the crossroads is the Manager's House, clearly a more upscale dwelling than most.

If you turn right at the crossroads and follow Furnace Road, you'll come to the most interesting section of this walk. Here, beyond an open grassy area are the remains of three iron furnaces built between 1766 and 1865. The oldest was about 25 feet high and produced iron during the Revolution; the stone walls you see are the foundations for the furnace's casting and wheelhouse. The other two were built during the Civil War, apparently reaching a height of 65 feet; the one to the north, oddly known as "Lucy" by the workers, was the last of Long Pond's furnaces to shut down, in 1882.

Continue past this last furnace to two waterwheels that harnessed the river to power the furnaces; follow the short uphill trail to the stone raceway that conducted the water to the waterwheel. A dirt road takes you from here to the remains of the Company Store, from which you follow the Furnace Road back to the Visitor Center to complete your loop. Before leaving Long Pond don't miss the museum with its various artifacts and displays of life here.

A visit to Ringwood Manor just up the road will give you a vastly different experience. The elegant Victorian-style house sits on a rise overlooking a small lake; surrounding it are grassy lawns and gardens and woods—some 33,000 acres in all. These are not the typical grounds of a country house; rather, they resemble an outdoor museum, with an eclectic collection of statuary and wrought-iron constructions strewn about the grass, along walkways, and near the house. (The house contains art works and period furnishings as well.) But, unlike most sculpture parks, the gardens here are home to many incidental marble ornamental sculptures and curious iron "confections" rather than primarily settings for art.

The present manor house was built in 1854 as the country seat of Cooper Hewitt. (The original, built by Robert Erskine, was a simple Colonial dwelling.) As the iron magnate's fortune was then considered among the country's largest, his house was suitably grand. His son-in-law, Abram S. Hewitt, and family decided to landscape a portion of Ringwood's many acres. The Hewitts developed the gardens by drawing upon the classical designs they had admired during their European travels, notably those of Versailles and the Villa d'Este. They set out formal and informal gardens, allées, terraces, rose arbors, ponds, and walls, many adorned with odd sculptures and relics of early American history. Large areas of pristine landscape were left in a natural state to emphasize the dramatic hilltop views. It is evident that Cooper had instilled in his daughter, Sarah Hewitt, a great respect for nature and conservation.

This is a truly intriguing estate, with ample room for walking and exploring and looking at the art and artifacts. There are no tags, no labels for identifying the art, and you are left on your own to imagine what they might be. You'll note the odd stone sphinxes that seem to have some sort of exotic motif (Mrs. Hewitt had several of them copied from the sphinxes at the Louvre), nymphs, and vaguely "classical" sculptured heads. One example is a classical statue representing Asia at one end of the main axis of the formal gardens; apparently it came from the bishop's palace at Avignon in France. The many wrought-iron works all around the manor house—among them iron lanterns that came from the governor's mansion in New York—seem perfectly appropriate to an iron magnate's home.

A striking iron decoration in front of the manor house is a section (or replica) of the famous chain that was stretched across the Hudson below West Point during the Revolution; near it is a cannon from Old Ironsides. And a particular oddity is the geometrically divided, stone-walled and terraced hillside above the manor. One of the most intriguing of these areas is a grove of straight and evenly spaced trees near the manor that creates an allée in which a series of identical torchères is laid out. Giving the impression of a vast green chessboard, this spot will delight anyone, including children, who will enjoy walking among the "figures." This spot is as eccentric as the giant iron gates that appear to lead nowhere in particular, other than to the lake below. In fact, these elegantly crafted gates—purchased by Abram Hewitt from Columbia University, his alma mater—do have a purpose: they mark the edge of the old Hasenclever Trail.

The Victorian-style mansion itself, with its porte cochere designed by none other than the noted architect Stanford White, was designated as a Registered National Historic Landmark in 1973. It includes more than fifty-one rooms (of which twenty-eight are bedrooms) and twenty-four fireplaces. Here you'll find quite an eclectic collection of furnishings in a variety of styles, from Louis XVI to Gothic Revival and Victorian. In this "summer home" the Hewitts entertained noted politicians, diplomats, and industrialists. Both inside and out, this remarkable estate, with its delightful relics from the past, recalls a fascinating era in the nation's history.

❧ IN THE VICINITY

Old Stone House Museum, 538 Island Road, Ramsey. This 1740 Dutch house and tavern, today a small hands-on museum featuring eighteenth-century artifacts. Telephone: 201-825-1126.

The Hermitage, 335 North Franklin Turnpike, Ho-Ho-Kus. During the Revolutionary War, the Hermitage (then a 1750 brownstone) was the home of Lieutenant Colonel Prevost and his wife, Theodosia. Here they hosted such illustrious people as James Monroe, Alexander Hamilton, General Lafayette, and Aaron Burr (who later married the lady of the house after she became widowed). The house was remodeled in 1847 in the Gothic Revival architectural style, as it appears today. A National Historic Landmark, the museum exhibits antique clothing (hundreds of women's gowns, fans, hand-made lace, and other items), as well as original furniture, antique maps, and memorabilia. Telephone: 201-445-8311.

8·
EDISON
NATIONAL
HISTORIC SITE

Edison Memorial Tower

*Exploring
an Extraordinary Legacy*

❧ HOW TO GET THERE

The Edison National Historic Site is located on Main Street and Lakeside Avenue in West Orange. From Route 280 take exit 10; turn right at the stop sign and left on Main Street. After about half a mile you'll see the site. Parking is on the left, and the laboratory on your right. Note: *Glenmont, Edison's private home, is located in nearby Llewellyn Park, about a mile away.*

❧ INFORMATION

As of this writing the Historic Site is closed for major renovation and plans to reopen sometime in 2006. The laboratory complex will be accessible via guided or self-guided tour; Glenmont, Edison's private home, will only be accessible via guided tour. Tour tickets for Glenmont available at the Visitor Center. Telephone: 973-736-0550. Web site: http://www.nps.gov/edis.

❧ New Jersey can be justly proud of its many illustrious native sons and daughters, but none stands out quite like Thomas Alva Edison. This extraordinary genius, whose surprising number of inventions—from the incandescent light bulb to the phonograph and motion pictures—changed the world forever, spent forty-four years at his laboratory and home in West Orange. It was here, from 1887 until his death in 1931, that he developed more than half of the 1,093 patents he received in his lifetime—more than anyone else. On this walk we take you to this fascinating complex, now the Edison National Historic Site, to explore the legacy of one of the most remarkable innovators of all time.

Though most of his inventions were created at this laboratory, some of Edison's most noted ones were developed in his previous lab at Menlo Park, earning him the nickname "the Wizard of Menlo Park." (Don't miss this site in nearby Edison; see below.) Among the four hundred or so patents that came out of Menlo Park was the miraculous incandescent light bulb, for which Edison is perhaps most remembered. True, he did not "invent" electricity per se, but through his vision he revolutionized its applicability, bringing it to millions of homes and offices for everyday use.

In West Orange, Edison set up a lab like no other. It is still considered the first modern research and development facility of its kind. This self-contained giant complex was operated by an army of workers (up to seven thousand at one point) and included labs for physics, chemistry, and metallurgy, a machine shop (for Edison's ongoing experiments), a pattern shop, and several factory buildings. Here he also developed the first Vitascope (which evolved into silent movies), the mimeograph, storage battery, and kinetiscope. He was interested in just about anything and everything: in the early 1900s this imaginative pioneer produced *The Great Train Robbery,* a short film that combined sound with moving images for the first time; it is regarded as a classic by film aficionados.

When the great man was not in his lab (which was seldom, much to his wife's chagrin), he could be found in his elegant estate about a mile away. Here at Glenmont, a large Queen Anne–style house on vast grounds, he and Mina Miller Edison hosted an endless number of noted public figures, from Marie Curie and Henry Ford to Charles Lindbergh and President Herbert Hoover. In his last years, Edison's home became his refuge while he worked in his home laboratory.

A visit to the Edison National Historic Site provides a fascinating insight into an American legend. Go first to the Visitor Center, which displays many of Edison's inventions and provides you with all the information you can possibly want. Then proceed to the laboratory compound, where you will discover (either through guided or self-guided tour) the many aspects of Edison's genius. Don't miss the Phonograph Room, the reproduction of the Black Maria (the movie studio he built on the grounds surrounding the labs), and the showing of *The Great Train Robbery,* among other highlights. Scattered about are more personal touches, too, such as Edison's tools at his workbench and his vintage coat hanging in its usual place. You'll also find a large wall clock in the library that indicates the exact time of Edison's death: 3:27 A.M. on October 18, 1931.

Glenmont can be visited only by guided tour (tickets available at the Visitor Center). Situated within Llewellyn Park, one of the nation's first planned residential developments (with access provided only to residents and authorized guests), it was home to the Edisons for many years, from 1857 on. In this large (and surprisingly dark) house of twenty-nine rooms you'll catch a glimpse of Edison's personal life, with myriad photos documenting events and friendships in addition to the anecdotes offered by the tour guide. Outside, in the lovely grounds, are the graves of Edison and his wife.

❧ IN THE VICINITY

Thomas Alva Edison Memorial Tower and Menlo Park Museum, 37 Christie Street, Edison. Free (but donations are welcome). Open Tuesday to Saturday, 10 A.M. to 4 P.M. Built in 1937 to mark Edison's ninety-first birthday, the tower and museum are situated on the very site of Edison's famous laboratory. Included are some of his inventions and products of his company (Thomas A. Edison Company), as well as much memorabilia. Telephone: 732-549-3299.

9·
FELTVILLE

Feltville

A Forgotten Utopian Village in the Watchung Reservation

❧ HOW TO GET THERE

New Jersey Turnpike to exit 14; go west on Route 78 to exit 44, and turn left onto Glenside Avenue. Feltville Village is less than a block down the road. Note: *If you are traveling east on Route 78, make a right onto Glenside Avenue from exit 44.*

❧ INFORMATION

You can visit Feltville at any time of the year; the few existing buildings are not open to the public (except for the newly renovated interpretive center in the church/general store), but you can walk around them. Parking is available on the premises; no entrance fee. Telephone: 908-789-3670. Web site: www.ucnj.org.

❧ There is much more to discover in the vast Watchung Reservation than you might expect. In fact, within these 2,000 acres of woodlands, trails, and wildflowers is an intriguing and little-known site, the remains of an abandoned mid-nineteenth-century village known as Feltville. When we first came here we were surprised to find—tucked away amid the trees, on a bluff overlooking a brook—a handful of houses that still looked habitable. Scattered along a winding stretch of road, they seemed to us mostly discarded and forlorn. Some had rustic Adirondack-style porches, appearing almost resortlike. We knew at once there had to be an interesting story behind these facades.

Feltville was apparently founded on utopian principles—to provide an ideal and self-sufficient and controlled environment for the improvement of the lives of its inhabitants. What makes this abandoned village especially interesting to us today is that it is one of the only (and the only one we could find) nineteenth-century utopian communities still standing in New Jersey. The better known Phalanx, near Red Hook, for example, has completely vanished.

In 1845 David Felt, a successful printer and stationery dealer from New York City, bought 760 acres of land in this secluded area. Here "the King" (as he was known by his employees) established the mill town of Feltville for the manufacture of paper and books. Wishing to create a contained community where his workers would both work and live, he built—in addition to the paper mill and a gristmill—cottages and dormitories, a school, church, several stores, and even a circulating library ("to improve their minds"). Concerned about the workers' spiritual well-being, he even hired an outside Unitarian minister, one Austin Craig, who would later found Antioch College in Ohio. For all of his lofty ideals and apparent benevolence, Felt ruled with an iron hand: he absolutely required that his workers live on the premises, where he could control their daily routines—even sounding a bell when he felt they should retire for the evening!

For fifteen years Feltville thrived, until for reasons still unclear Felt sold the community and left town forever. After several takeovers from one owner to the next, including a manufacturer of patent medicines known as the "Sasparilla King," the town was transformed into a summer resort, more attractively renamed Glenside Park. It was at this point, in the 1880s, that porches and dormer roofs were added to existing dwellings, changing their simple colonial look into something more fanciful and Victorian. Among its amenities, the retreat offered lawn tennis, golf, fishing, croquet, and even electric lights, and functioned until 1916, when vacationers started going elsewhere. The property was eventually bought by the county for parkland. Today its 120 acres have become the site of something called "Operation Archaeology," a Union County program that introduces historic archeology to young students, giving them hands-on field experience. Montclair University has also been carrying out on-site excavations to examine the life of the town and its inhabitants.

Though Feltville once had as many as thirty-five houses and structures, only ten survive; of these, three are presently occupied. Because the structures are fragile, visitors are not allowed to walk up onto porches, except in the case of the recently refurbished interpretive center in the Church/Store Building. Further restoration of existing buildings in the park is now underway.

The park offers a self-guided walking tour and descriptive brochure (available at the interpretive center); the recommended one-mile walk begins and ends at the parking lot off Glenside Avenue. (Note that a one-room schoolhouse once stood where you now park your car.) As you walk through this now quiet site, you can try to imagine its past, when it was a lively and industrious place, bustling with activity.

From the parking lot walk down Cataract Hollow Road; if you wish to visit the village cemetery first (as suggested in the brochure) make a left at the first trail crossing and wind your way down the ravine, following the signs. (You can also save exploring the cemetery until the end of your walk.) Here members of the Willcocks family are buried. Peter Willcocks, the area's first European settler, came here before the Revolutionary War and built a dam across Blue Brook, and a sawmill; Felt bought his land from Willcocks's descendants. Of the five tombstones still standing, only one (at the far right) is original.

Retrace your steps up to Cataract Hollow Road, turn left, and walk to the first house. This rather large building (it was originally much smaller) served as Felt's business office. Walk to the next building down the road. Recently restored, it was once the general store and church and serves as the interpretive center. We are told that the steeple was added well after the building was used as a church.

Continue along the road, as it winds around, and you'll come upon a group of four houses. These were used by the workers and their families. Each house was divided up to accommodate as many as four families, with separate entrances. After the village became a resort, the houses were converted into single units.

Walk farther along the road until you see a bridle trail along a stone wall; go down the trail until you reach Blue Brook, the site of the former mill and the center of activity in Feltville. (In the era of Glenside Park, the mill was used as a stable for cattle.) Go back up to the road, turn left, and you'll see three little cottages. Apparently these smaller dwellings accommodated couples who had no children.

Your last stop is Masker's Barn, at the end of Cataract Hollow Road. This building, dating from the 1880s, was used as a barn for the horses that transported resort guests; today it houses Operation Archeology (the site of their dig is nearby). Retrace your steps, walking back to the parking lot.

If after this "history walk" you still wish to walk farther, there are many miles of hiking trails right here, within the Watchung Reservation. (See the park brochure.) The park also offers bridle trails, designated areas for spotting wildlife, a nature and science center, planetarium, and more.

✿ IN THE VICINITY

The Museum of Early Trades and Crafts, Main Street and Green Village Road, Madison, features eighteenth- and nineteenth-century crafts. Telephone: 973-377-2982.

The Littell-Lord Farmhouse, 31 Horseshoe Road, Berkley Heights, is a pre-Revolutionary War farmstead. Telephone: 908-464-0961.

Woodruff House/Eaton Store Museum, 111 Conant Street, Hillside. This site includes the 1735 house and community store, as well as a barn and miscellaneous artifacts. Telephone: 908-352-9270.

Merchants and Drovers Tavern, 1632 St. Georges Avenue, Rahway. This twenty-five-room tavern (dating from circa 1795) was a stagecoach stop between New York and Philadelphia. Costumed interpreters will explain it all to you. Telephone: 732-381-0441.

Whippany Railway Museum, Route 10W and Whippany Road, Whippany. This is a restored freight house with historic trains, memorabilia, a coal yard, wooden water tank, and more. Telephone: 973-887-8177.

10·
HISTORIC
SPEEDWELL

Speedwell Village

A Village of Inventions

❧ HOW TO GET THERE

Take Route 287 to exit 36 and follow signs to Morristown. From downtown Morristown, take Speedwell Avenue (Route 202 north) for about one mile. Turn right onto Cory Road and left into the Speedwell parking lot.

❧ INFORMATION

Historic Speedwell is located at 333 Speedwell Avenue (Route 202) in Morristown. Open Wednesday through Saturday, 10 A.M. to 5 P.M., and Sunday noon to 5 P.M., from April through October. Telephone: 973-540-0211; Web site: www.speedwell.org.

❧ Historic Speedwell represents more than you might think. At first glance, this historic landmark appears to be just a charming group of vintage houses and barns on a grassy slope, like many other rural spots of eighteenth- and nineteenth-century America. What you see is a pleasantly quiet and uncommercial place, an inviting little oasis of just a few acres surrounded by a bustling area. In fact, this was once a busy site with a surprising array of creative activity involving ironworks and related inventions. But most remarkably, it was here that the first successful public demonstration of the telegraph actually took place, a fact not widely known.

A forge powered by a dam of the Whippany River had been in existence near the site for some years, even supplying General Washington's army with munitions. The enterprising Stephen Vail, seeing a good commercial opportunity, built the Speedwell Ironworks there during the early 1800s. The ironworks prospered and Vail (who had become a judge) bought more property, including a factory for cotton weaving. This land and its adjoining farm became Judge Vail's Homestead Farm.

The story now shifts to Vail's elder son, Alfred. Upon entering New York University in 1832, Alfred met the great Samuel F. B. Morse, then a professor of fine arts there. Morse, a very fine (though commercially unsuccessful) artist-turned-inventor had been experimenting persistently with the telegraph for some years. He envisioned an electromagnet that could record information over distances: "I see no reason why intelligence may not be transmitted instantaneously by electricity," he said. Realizing that Morse needed financial and technical help to achieve his goal, Alfred (himself an inventor) offered his expertise, as well as his father's shop in the ironworks to develop the invention further and eventually conduct the experiment. On January 6, 1838, after months of preparation, the demonstration that changed the world finally took place. With an assembled group (including the skeptical Judge Vail) and three miles of copper wire looped about the walls of the room, Morse and Alfred succeeded in transmitting Judge Vail's message, "If you can send this and Professor Morse can read it at the other end, I shall be convinced." The judge was indeed convinced, and the duo's amazing success marked the birth of today's telegraph. Eventually a new register recording dots and lines on a piece of paper was developed, and the "Morse code" came to be. And, in 1843, the first telegraph line, between Washington and Baltimore, was built.

In 1873, the ironworks were moved to Brooklyn; years later some of the buildings burned. Eventually "Historic Speedwell" was formed, officially opening its doors in 2002 as part of the Morris County Parks Commission.

The structures you see today at Speedwell were not all built on the premises: the main ones—the Factory, Homestead Carriage House and Wheel House, and the Vail House—were part of the original homestead and ironworks, while others threatened elsewhere by demolition and urban renewal were later brought here from other locations. The buildings are all marked (very discretely) for easy identification and are close together, with stretches of grass in between. The ambience here is lovely—low-key and rustic. Though the entire property is no more than a few acres (7.5), there is plenty to see and read about as you walk in and out of buildings, enjoying a variety of fascinating exhibits.

Before starting your walk, stop at the white-frame Visitor Center, the **L'Hommedieu House** (#4); here you can pick up a self-guided walking tour and other information, as well as arrange for a guided tour of the Factory Building to see a demonstration of the early telegraph. This building, dating from the 1820s, was originally located in another part of Morristown.

The **Ford Cottage** (#1), dating from about 1800, was also moved here from surrounding Morristown. This delightful little house with its small paned windows is not open to the public as of this writing, but can be admired from the outside.

Facing the cottage is a large red building with irregular windows. This is the **Factory Building** (#2), built by Stephen Vail in the late 1820s to accommodate a cotton mill that never came to be. Instead, this building was the site of a sawmill, gristmill, and other business activities. And, of course, it was here that Morse's famous experiment took place. (The existing wonderful old beams still show the nails used in stringing the wire around the room.) When we last visited we were told that the building is scheduled for renovation in the near future. We hope any improvements will retain the genuine atmosphere of this wonderful old place with all its objects and memorabilia.

The attached **Wheelhouse** (#3) contains a massive twenty-four-foot over-shot wheel. An earlier waterwheel was originally built here to generate power for the cotton mill; when the mill never materialized, the wheel was used to power a bone-grinding mill and small gristmill; the mechanisms of both are on display in the Homestead Carriage House. The existing waterwheel, one of the largest in operation in New Jersey, was actually built by Stephen Vail in 1848 (it was cast at his ironworks) and is also about to be restored. You'll be fascinated watching it in operation.

The **Moses Estey House** (#5), another import from Morristown, dates from the late 1700s. As of now, this house is not open to visitors.

The **Granary** (#6) houses hand-crafted wooden farm tools and other items as part of a permanent exhibit.

The **Carriage House** (#7), dating from 1849, offers lectures, workshops, and various other programs.

The **Homestead Carriage House** (#8), one of the main buildings original to the site, contains wonderful exhibits of the Speedwell Ironworks. Here you can learn about Vail's various business enterprises, including the creation of the steam engine for the SS *Savannah*, the first transatlantic steam-powered ship in the world. There is a great deal to see here, and you will want to linger for a bit.

Finally you'll come to the **Vail House** (#9), the Vail family home from the 1820s until the mid-1900s. Hanging in the central hallway are family portraits painted by Morse in 1837.

❧ IN THE VICINITY

The Morristown region is one of the most historic in the state. We have included several other nearby sites besides those below that are worth visiting: see Jockey Hollow (walk 12) and Acorn Hall (page 59).

Fosterfields Living Historical Farm, 73 Kahdena Road, Morristown. This hundred-year-old farm complex,built by Paul Revere's grandson and today listed as a National Register Historic Site, sits on two hundred bucolic acres and contains farm animals, old machinery, and a lovely farmhouse with period furniture. Here, costumed staff will show you what it was like to live on a farm at the time, how livestock was raised, and what methods were used to grow crops; they will even encourage you to participate in activities such as churning butter and cleaning harnesses. This is a great place for the kids (schoolchildren are often brought here). Telephone: 973-362-7645.

Stickley Museum at Craftsman Farms, Manor Lane, 2352 Route 10W, Morris Plains. This National Historic Landmark was the home and workshop of Gustave Stickley, designer of Mission furniture and Craftsman homes, which were part of the Arts and Crafts Movement between 1900 and 1916. Telephone: 973-540-1165.

11·
PYRAMID MOUNTAIN

Tripod Rock on Pyramid Mountain

A Leni-Lenape Legacy

❧ HOW TO GET THERE

Take I-287 to exit 44 to the center of Boonton. Turn right onto Route 511 (Boonton Avenue) and travel 3.3 miles to the Pyramid Mountain Natural and Historic Area. Pick up a map at the Visitor Center and look for blue blazes at access trail.

❧ INFORMATION

The park is open daily, dawn to dusk. Free. Guided trail walks available through the Visitor Center. Telephone: 973-334-3130; Web site: www.morrisparks.net/parks/pyrmtnmain.htm.

❧ This walk on Pyramid Mountain Natural Historic Area takes you through a spectacular and rugged landscape of 1,000 acres to Tripod Rock, a scenic as well as significant site. Tripod Rock, one of the most massive boulders in the East, is thought to have been the site of Native American summer solstice observations. This giant rock has been balancing on three smaller rocks for some 15,000 years, and today Tripod Rock still looks as it must have looked to the Leni-Lenape who, according to legend, worshiped there.

The Leni-Lenape, who inhabited the region stretching from the southern Catskills through New Jersey and parts of Delaware and eastern Pennsylvania, were a peace-loving people. Their name, from the Unami dialect, means "common," "ordinary," or "real" peoples. William Penn, who wrote about them and even learned their language, found them to have "a deep natural sagacity [to] say little, but what they speak is fervent and elegant." Giovanni da Verrazano, who came here even earlier, said they were "some of the sweetest, gentlest people he'd ever met on any of his voyages." Part of the Algonquin nation, they lived under constant threat of warfare from their neighbors, the Iroquois, and lived by farming, hunting, and fishing. They were deeply religious. It is thought that they celebrated the solstices at the site we will visit. It is still a popular spot for celebrations of the solstices by non-Indians.

The walk we propose is a circular loop of about 3 miles on Pyramid Mountain (a hunting and fishing area for the Leni-Lenape) to Tripod Rock, following the blue trail through a dense forest. It begins with an easy climb up stone steps. You will pass wildflowers in springtime and autumn, including the Joe-pye weed, a tall plant that grows to the height of a person; it has pinkish purple blossoms, from which the Leni-Lenape extracted a balm to treat typhoid fever. Among many other wildflowers you might also see jewelweed, which the Lenape used to soothe poison ivy. Soon you will catch your first glimpse of boulders known as glacial erratics, which were created by the melting of the Wisconsin Glacier some 15,000 years ago. Particularly lovely in June, this area is covered with blossoming mountain laurel. The blue trail is somewhat arduous and steep, and is strewn with boulders. (Wear stout shoes!)

You will pass Lucy's Overlook, a ledge from which you can spot migrating birds, with views of Stony Brook Mountain to the west. The blue-blazed trail intersects with a white trail, and the latter leads to Tripod Rock (also called Three Pillar Rock). You won't miss Tripod Rock, a 200-ton boulder that rests precariously upon three small rocks. This extraordinary rock is described by archeologists as the focal point of an ancient calendar site. You can watch the summer solstice sunset through a gap between the stones, a solar observation long celebrated at this site. You can easily picture the Lenape engaging in their ancient rituals here.

Continuing on your loop walk, retrace your steps to the intersection with the blue trail, and go right, to reach Bear Rock, another massive boulder from the Ice Age. It is perched at the edge of a large swamp, surrounded by woods. Nearby is a waterfall. Follow the trail downward toward the parking lot. You will pass another footnote to history on your right: the tiny foundation ruins of the Morgan Place, a hideout for a dangerous clan of nineteenth-century robbers who raided the Boonton region.

❀ IN THE VICINITY

Mount Tabor, Route 53, off Route 80. On a completely different theme, visit nearby Mount Tabor, a historic area of Victorian gingerbread houses and historic public buildings. Telephone: 973-586-1564.

❀ ADDITIONAL SITES OF SIMILAR INTEREST

For additional Leni-Lenape sites (but farther afield), you can visit the following.

Garrett Mountain, behind Lambert Castle and the Paterson Falls (see walk 1), both of which are known to have been important. On Garrett Mountain there are three rock caves, including two just behind Lambert Castle. The Lenape are known to have driven deer in a northeastern direction, toward the Great Falls. The area there is still known as Deer Leap.

The **Lenape Village** in Waterloo, near Stanhope (see walk 15).

Pahaquarra Archaeological Site, Harwick Township in the Delaware Water Gap National Recreation Area. This site, excavated during the 1960s and 1970s, has yielded interesting information concerning the lifestyle of the Lenape, including the role of women and children. Apparently, Lenape women (and children) cultivated small plots of beans, maize, squash, and sunflowers, which contributed more food to the community than that provided through hunting and fishing. Telephone: 570-588-2432.

12·
JOCKEY HOLLOW

Jockey Hollow Encampment

Woodland Trails
and Soldiers' Huts

❀ HOW TO GET THERE

Take Route 287 to exit 30B; turn right at traffic light onto Route 202 north, then left onto Tempe Wick Road. Drive approximately 2 miles and look for Jockey Hollow on your right.

❀ INFORMATION

Open daily 9 A.M. to 5 P.M., except major holidays. Telephone: 973-539-4030; Web site: www.nps.gov/morr.

❀ Jockey Hollow, one of the most inviting places we know that relates to the Revolutionary War, is today a serenely beautiful historic park of hardwood forests and wildflowers, meadows, and brooks. When you first come here, you might find it hard to imagine that it was once the site of a major military encampment. In fact, some 12,000 troops of General Washington's Continental Army camped on these hills during the winter of 1779–80 under the most arduous conditions. But history does seem to come alive here, and you do gain a sense of this harsh chapter of the war. Along the well-marked trails are stops and interpretive signs to help you locate, for example, the reconstructed soldiers' huts or the field where military ceremonies and daily training took place; and within the park is also a charming little cottage with a surrounding garden that gives you a taste of farm life during that time. By the time you leave, perhaps you will have experienced on some level this poignant time in American history.

As the winter of 1779 approached, General Washington knew he needed a place to house the Continental Army. Morristown, chosen for its strategic location (near the Watchung Mountains, which would provide cover from the British troops), became a center of the American Revolution. Washington set up his headquarters in an elegant private house in town and chose Jockey Hollow as the encampment for his army. Though it was in fact several miles away (and a good hour on horseback), the area was a rich forestland that could provide the timber needed to build more than one thousand huts.

As the men arrived in early December, they found the ground already frozen and snowcovered and could barely build their cabins fast enough to provide the needed shelter. The huts were constructed in rows of eight on the hillsides, with as many as twelve men in each hut, in very cramped quarters. Conditions were grueling in this coldest of winters with its record twenty-eight snowfalls. There was not enough food or warm clothing to go around. Washington wrote that his men sometimes went without bread for five or six days and "ate every kind of horse food but hay." There was also an epidemic of smallpox, which resulted in the deaths of hundreds (the Jockey Hollow cemetery contains graves of many who died here). And, not surprising, all these miseries resulted in mutinies on the part of the besieged soldiers: the first, a brief one in spring of 1780, involved the Connecticut brigade and lasted a short time; the second, much more destructive, took place in January 1781, after Washington had left Morristown, and included some two thousand troops who eventually marched on to Philadelphia.

A walk through Jockey Hollow will give you a fascinating insight into the army's struggle to survive. Before starting your walk, stop at the Visitor Center to pick up your ticket and self-guided walking information. All trails (there are four main ones of varying lengths, as well as connecting roadways and short footpaths, some 27 miles total) are well indicated on the map provided. We especially recommend the yellow trail, which is about 2.25 miles long and starts nearby, but you can follow others as well, as they intersect. From the Visitor Center follow the gravel path for a first stop at Tempe Wick Farm (ask one of the guides at the Center to take you inside the cottage to see its quite spartan living quarters). This pretty little house was once part of a 1,400-acre farm belonging to the prosperous Wick family. Their daughter Temperance—"Tempe"—was a legendary character who bravely confronted soldiers who were trying to steal her horse; she raced away from them and dashed home, hiding the animal in her bedroom for several weeks. When the encampment was established, the farm became the headquarters of General Arthur St. Clair. The cottage has been carefully restored, along with its vegetable and herb garden and orchard, and provides a delightful glimpse into the life of a comfortable farm family of that era.

Walk past the barn in back and turn onto a paved road. At the fork look for yellow markers, and follow the trail through the woods. Imagine how desolate this landscape must have looked after its many oaks and chestnuts and walnuts were cut down for timber! Now a forest mostly of white ash, black locust, and beech, it is unusually well maintained and you can easily see through the trees. The trail runs alongside Cemetery Road (to your left) and intersects a few paths along the way. It eventually turns to the right, and you come to a vast clearing; on the hillside above, called Sugar Loaf Hill, are five of the original two hundred soldiers' huts that once stood in rows along here (rebuilt in the 1930s). It was at this site that the Pennsylvania Brigade of about two thousand men camped during the fateful winter of 1779–80. You'll find interpretive signs with interesting information about it all and will want to linger here for some time. We recommend climbing up the hill to visit these rustic constructions, both inside and outside. Each measured fourteen by sixteen feet and contained simple basic furniture also built by the soldiers. As you might expect, the common soldiers were assigned to the exposed huts in front, leaving the more protected huts in back to the officers.

From here it's a short distance to the Grand Parade (you can either continue on the yellow trail or follow the Grand Parade Road). You can well imagine the military ceremonies and parades that took place in this big open field, as well as the daily drills and training. Visiting dignitaries would sometimes be invited to witness events involving the entire army, which must have been quite a lively scene. One of these important visitors, the Marquis de Lafayette, came to announce in the spring of 1780 that France would soon send soldiers to help the American cause, much to Washington's great relief. Don't miss the interpretive displays describing the many activities that took place here or nearby, including the mutiny of the Connecticut brigade mentioned above.

Continue on the yellow trail, which crosses Grand Parade Road at this point, or Jockey Hollow Road, and go up a long hill that eventually circles back to Wick Farm. Along the way you'll find more signs and interpretive displays explaining what you're seeing, as well as markers inviting you to take a detour here and there.

✿ IN THE VICINITY

Fort Nonsense, off Chestnut Street, near the intersection of Western Avenue and Anne Street, Morristown. This unusual fort came about in May 1777, when, for no apparent reason, Washington ordered the troops to build a 600-foot-high earthen fort overlooking Morristown. Was it just to keep them occupied (as the legend claims), or to be able to see the approaching enemy? The fort has in fact spectacular views in all directions, including New York City to the east. Telephone: 973-539-2085.

Acorn Hall, 68 Morris Avenue, Morristown. This Victorian house in the Italianate style contains many of its original furnishings, in addition to antique toys and gadgets. Surrounding it is a lovely lawn and Victorian garden with gazebo. Telephone: 973-267-3465.

Schuyler-Hamilton House, 5 Olyphant Place, Morristown. This colonial house has the distinction of having been the site where the courtship between Alexander Hamilton and Betsey Schuyler took place—hence its name. Telephone: 973-267-4039.

Macculoch Hall, 45 Macculloch Avenue, Morristown. Telephone: 973-538-2404.

The Middlebrook Winter Encampment of Washington's Army, Cedarcrest Road, Bridgewater. At this spot, the site of Washington's two encampments, the first official thirteen-star flag was flown. Telephone: 908-218-1281.

13·
COOPER MILL
AND THE
BLACK RIVER

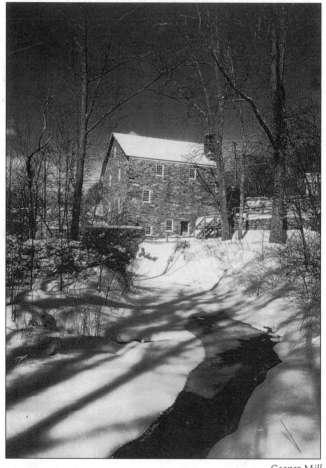

Cooper Mill

History amid Wooded Splendor

❧ HOW TO GET THERE

Take Route 80 west to Route 206 south to Chester; turn right onto Route 513 (Route 24), go 1.2 miles to Cooper Mill on your left.

❧ INFORMATION

Cooper Mill is located within the Black River County Park, near the side of the road. It is open on weekends May through October, 10 A.M. to 5 P.M., and Tuesday through Friday during July and August. Tours and demonstrations of the workings of the mill, given by the staff in period costume, are offered every half hour through 4 P.M., but call first to reserve, as these are popular events. The trails are open year-round, dawn to dusk. Telephone: 908-879-5463; Web site: www.morrisparks.net/parks/coopermillmain.htm.

❧ The Black River Valley in Morris County is endowed with unusually pretty scenery and a great diversity of plants and wildlife within a well-protected wilderness. The river itself is only 12 miles long; but in those few miles it changes dramatically from a sluggish stream to roaring waters, as it winds through hardwood forests filled with rhododendrons, meadows dotted with wildflowers, and a hemlock ravine. It is difficult to imagine that this unspoiled natural area was once an important industrial site rather than the scenic parkland it is today. In fact, since the eighteenth century, settlers began to harvest the region's special resources, eventually with considerable profit. They used the river to power forges and mills, one of which—Cooper Mill, one of the oldest and most picturesque in the state—has been recently restored. They found iron ore as they dug mines along the shoreline; and they constructed a railroad to transport the iron to nearby furnaces.

In this outing we explore some of the area's historic heritage. We stop first at Cooper Mill, then go on an inviting forest path that follows the river, where the railroad once passed on its way to nearby iron mines. This 3.6-mile out-and-back trail, which begins just a few steps below the stone mill, connects to the Kay Environmental Center, an interesting place to visit as well (see below). Both are located within the 510-acre Black River County Park, near Hacklebarney Park. You can leave your car right at the lot in front of the mill, then walk to the Visitor Center; this historic building was once the home of Abram Cooper. Here you can pick up information and trail maps; the Center also has exhibits relating to social, technical, and agricultural aspects of life in the Black River area during the eighteenth and nineteenth centuries.

Cooper Mill was built in 1826 by Nathan Cooper on the site of an earlier flour mill, dating from 1760. The site was chosen because the river at this point drops precipitously into the gorge, generating great power. The large, four-story mill thrived, grinding wheat, corn, and other grains, and played a key role in the community and the region's industrial development. It was considered quite an innovative marvel in its day, as it used new technologies to make milling more energy efficient and profitable. The mill today operates in the same way: for example, only two cups of water are needed to make its sixteen-foot-high waterwheel spin, and it can grind eight hundred pounds of flour per hour.

Now a living museum, Cooper Mill is the only restored water-powered gristmill in the state. It was opened to the public after restoration in 1978. You can watch the giant waterwheel and power shafts at work turning the massive grind stones (great for children to see), or enjoy demonstrations of blacksmithing and stone dressing. The museum also offers special events, such as traditional colonial reenactments. Bear in mind that these are often well attended (check ahead in case you would prefer being there at a quieter time).

After your visit, walk down the stairs at the south side of the mill and find the blue-blaze trail. This small path proceeds toward the rushing water and climbs up a raised embankment, a remnant of the railroad era. The Hacklebarney branch of the High Bridge Railroad (later the Central Railroad of New Jersey) once passed by here; it served the iron mines along the Black River as it transported the ore to the nearby Chester Furnace. Though the mines had existed in the area since the late 1700s, it wasn't until the 1880s that they reached their peak of productivity. At the turn of the century other ore deposits, less expensive to mine, were discovered farther afield, and the railroad line was abandoned.

Continue walking on the narrow-gauge rail bed for the first mile or so. You'll find yourself in a woodland of tall oaks and tulip trees, flowering shrubs, and wildflowers. The river swirls around large black boulders, making a roaring sound, and widens into a little pond with water lilies and ducks, behind a stone dam. This nineteenth-century mill complex, including forge and machine shops, generated electricity for the nearby Kay estate in the 1920s.

When you've gone a bit over a mile you come to a junction where a sign points to the Kay Environmental Center (eight-tenths of a mile ahead). For an easier and shorter walk, continue on the blue-blazed path to the Center; your other option is to explore the Black River Gorge hemlock ravine—an additional 1.5 miles—which is truly glorious, but quite rugged. (Consult your trail guide.) Either way, you eventually find your way to the open meadows surrounding the Center. Their flowering dogwoods, shrubs, and wildflowers are especially spectacular in spring. A long, circular trail winds around the grass, enabling you to enjoy this lovely spot (and its many birds and butterflies) more fully.

This was once the 223-acre estate of Elizabeth Kay, a remarkable naturalist and benefactor. In 1994 it was given to the county to be used as an environmental center; the Kay Environmental Center was created so that "each day would bring a new wonder and challenge to learn." There is much to see and explore here in terms of nature—guided walks, exhibits, symposia; but bear in mind that you still have to walk back to Cooper Mill.

14·
THE SUSSEX
BRANCH
RAIL TRAIL

Early train travel

Old Mines, Bridges, and Ruins

❀ HOW TO GET THERE

From Route 80, take exit 25 to Route 206 north. After about a mile turn left onto Route 604 (Waterloo Road). Go one mile toward Allamuchy State Park and leave your car at the parking lot directly opposite Continental Drive. The entrance to the Rail Trail is marked.

❀ INFORMATION

Though the length of this portion of the trail is about 15 miles (from Alla-muchy State Park to Lafayette, north of Sparta), six more miles have been recently added, all the way to Branchville, making its full length some 21 miles. Needless to say, you can commit to as much of the trail as you like. (Check a trail map for other return options, in case you prefer not to retrace your steps; maps are available at the post office in the town of Andover, or you can send away for one through the Kittatinny Valley State Park at P.O. Box 621, Andover, NJ 07821.) You can also access the trail at the towns of Andover, Newton, Hamtpon, and Lafayette. No fee. Open year-round, dawn to dusk. For further information, contact Kittatinny Valley State Park at 973-786-6445 or check out www.state.nj.us/dep/parksandforests/parks/kittval.html on the Internet.

❀ Rail trails offer some of the most pleasurable walks we know of in our region. Most are nice and flat and topped with soft cinder dirt (therefore, easy on the feet); they provide a variety of landscapes that can change rapidly, say, from woods to farmland; and, of special interest to us, many are of historic significance, too. In the nineteenth and early twentieth centuries these were the railroad beds of the trains that crossed New Jersey, as they transported people and goods. Along these paths you can still find remnants of the bygone railroad era, from ruins of old stations or ice-houses that serviced the lines in their heyday, to bridges or the remains of nearby iron mines.

Of the many rail trails we have discovered on our forays around the state, one of our favorites is the Sussex Branch Rail Trail. This delightful trail is both historic and scenic, beautifully set with lakes, woodlands, swamps, meadows, and an occasional village here and there. In fact, you won't want to turn around and go home on this one, even though this section of it runs for almost 15 miles. (As we noted above, the entire length of the Sussex Branch Rail Trail is now about 21 miles and there is talk of making it even longer.) The passing scene ranges from burbling brooks way below the walkway to isolated lakes (some were once sources for cutting ice), to people's backyards, to the wonderful "Hole in the Wall," a bridge dating from the mid-nineteenth century.

The rail line, Sussex County's first railroad, was built in the mid-nineteenth century by iron magnate Abrahm S. Hewitt of Long Pond and Ringwood fame (see walk 7). Originally a very narrow gauge rail line only 7 miles long (known a the Sussex Mine Railroad), it was a mule-powered operation preceding the steam railroad, designed to access the iron ore in the town of Andover. The ore carts would then be transported to the port of Waterloo on the Morris Canal, then loaded onto barges headed for the Delaware River. By 1864 the line had been extended, and the Sussex Railroad went on to become a coveted property, acquired in the 1880s by the Lackawanna Railroad, becoming the Delaware, Lackawanna and Western Railroad.

The Lackawanna also transported milk and other agrarian produce to major cities, a lucrative activity it continued long after the Andover furnace was shut down. Eventually time ran out for the rural line, as it was excluded from the plan that created the giant Conrail in the 1970s. Like other small tracks, it languished in weedy oblivion. Finally in 1982 it was sold to the New Jersey Department of Environmental Protection; its tracks removed, it was converted into a walking/hiking/biking trail, and is now managed by the State Park Service. Today, as you walk along this path, you can't help but wonder what it was like in its original form and how many people depended on the railroad.

The well-marked trail begins right near the parking lot; follow the gate into the woods. After you've walked a short distance (less than a quarter of a mile), on your right you'll see Jefferson Lake, once a source for cutting ice, with an icehouse siding that still stands. Before refrigeration, ice harvesting was an important industry for railroads. They would set up their enterprise on a freshwater lake, where they would cut and store the ice before transporting it to nearby towns during the summer months.

The trail continues to Cranberry Lake, which at the turn of the century was an elegant resort community serviced by the railroad—in fact, the Lackawanna actually built the resort. Here you can find a parallel railroad grade, which was part of the original Sussex Mine Railroad.

After a mile you leave the deep woods and enter beautiful open meadows and cornfields, a great spot for bird watching, by the way. Continuing on the trail, at about 3 miles from its starting point you'll come to the intriguing remains of a small house, with trees growing inside. A bit farther along is the picturesque arch bridge known as "The Hole in the Wall," installed in 1853 to connect Route 206 and Whitehall Hill Road.

Some of the points of interest you'll come upon if you continue walking include the immense Lackawanna Cutoff, a 28-mile railroad project built to handle local flooding with concrete viaducts and massive fill (this huge dig resulted in the creation of a few ponds); a causeway that divides two bodies of water, with swans and other water fowl present; remains of stone walls in a wooded area, a former farm; a stone house (at mile 10), once a passenger station featured in archive photos; and the remains of the only wooden bridge on the Lackawanna Railroad (at mile 11.5).

In addition to these odd examples of railroad memorabilia, you'll find wonderful natural diversity on this trail—from the mysterious woodlands around Jefferson Lake, to the swamps of the Newton Meadows, to the farmland surrounding the quaint town of Lafayette, where you can take in scenic vistas of the Paulinskill River and its tributaries. One can imagine passengers of the Lackawanna enjoying much of the same landscape years ago as they traveled through the countryside.

❉ ADDITIONAL SITES OF SIMILAR INTEREST

The Sterling Hill Mining Museum, 30 Plant Street, Ogdensburg. This underground museum features the history of mining in the region, including artifacts and minerals. Tours are available. Telephone: 973-209-7212.

The Picatinny Arsenal, Route 15, Jefferson Township. This is the site of a large forge that produced cannon balls for the Continental Army during the Revolutionary War. Telephone: 201-724-2797.

Mount Hope Historical Park, in nearby Morris County, just off Route 80 at exit 35. Once a booming iron mining and processing site, this tract now includes 3 miles of trails where you walk past subsistence pits (large holes created by abandoned mine shafts) and other remains of early twentieth century mining. Telephone: 973-326-7600.

15·
WATERLOO VILLAGE

Waterloo Village

*A Walk through a
Nineteenth-Century Canal Town*

❀ HOW TO GET THERE

Take Route 80 to exit 25 in Stanhope; go north 1 mile on Route 206, then turn left on Waterloo Road and continue for about 2.5 miles, following signs for the village.

❀ INFORMATION

Waterloo Village is open to the general public from May to the end of October, Wednesday through Sunday, 10 A.M. to 6 P.M. Because the village is quite a school-trip attraction, you are best off visiting on the weekends. Telephone: 973-347-0900; Web site: www.waterloovillage.org.

❀ Set alongside the long-abandoned Morris Canal that runs parallel to the Musconetcong River and Waterloo Lake just beyond, Waterloo Village is a marvelously picturesque place to explore while catching a glimpse into the life of a nineteenth-century rural community. This charming preserved village includes homesteads, blacksmiths, taverns, general stores, a nice canal house, and a sawmill—among the thirty-odd structures on its winding lanes. Though a few of the buildings are closed to the public, you can visit many others as you follow a self-guided tour available at the entrance. Some feature artisans (blacksmiths, weavers, or candle makers) demonstrating colonial crafts, while others offer exhibits with costumed guides on hand. Historic reenactments are also popular village events. Yet, despite all this activity and a good number of visitors much of the time (among them many groups of schoolchildren), you'll find Waterloo to be a delightful and quite peaceful place, combining natural pleasures with a real feel for history.

The site itself has been inhabited for thousands of years, since the Leni-Lenape Indians first settled in the region. A seventeenth-century Lenape village has recently been re-created on a small island in Waterloo Lake to mark these historic roots. Here you can see a reconstructed village of huts, dug-out canoes, a community longhouse, and fascinating tools and crafts. Signs describing the life of these Native Americans are posted en route.

With the discovery of iron ore during the eighteenth century, a forge was built here, which processed pig iron from a nearby furnace; originally Loyalist-owned, Andover Forge was confiscated by the Americans in 1778 and supplied armaments to the Continental Army.

Waterloo did not exist as a real village until the 1830s, with the opening of the Morris Canal, a monumental engineering achievement, extending from the Delaware River at Phillipsburg to the Hudson in Newark. Literally formed overnight as an important inland port with a guardlock and one of twenty-three inclined planes of the entire length of the canal, it grew very quickly. Most of the structures that still stand here today were built during those early prosperous years—the gristmill, stagecoach inn and tavern, blacksmith shop, canal house, and several elegant homes among them.

The coming of the railroad in midcentury (in this case, the Sussex and Morris & Essex) ultimately changed Waterloo's fortunes: this more efficient mode of transportation eventually put the canal out of business, and many surrounding towns with it. The village became a more or less deserted town; finally, years later, it underwent extensive restoration and, in 1964, was open to the public under the auspices of an arts foundation. Waterloo, now listed in the National Register of Historic Places, is a fascinating place to explore.

Your walk through this restored village and along the scenic towpath of the Morris Canal will take you through more than a century of American history. After you park your car, pick up the self-guided walking tour information at the entrance. The map indicates some thirty-three stops, clearly shown and described, all of which you can see or not, depending on your interests and time. Below we note only those you should not miss.

A good place to start is the stately **Waterloo United Methodist Church** (#1 on the map), which has not missed a service since it was built in 1859. (The public is still welcome to attend Sunday service.) From here continue your walk along the waterways, enjoying the picturesque views and crossing over little bridges and intersections of the three bodies of water that border the village.

The **Canal House** (#3) dates from Waterloo's iron manufacturing times during the eighteenth century. Here village workers were offered accommodation.

The **General Store** (#5, also called Smith's General Store), a stone building situated right on the bank of the Morris Canal, was built in 1831. Here canal boats loaded with grain, lumber, wood, coal, or iron ore would routinely glide right up to the store to leave off their supplies.

The store, a very successful enterprise, was managed by the prominent Smith family, who also built several of the private houses in the village.

The **Homestead** (#6), a horse barn on the iron plantation that preceded the village, eventually became the home of Peter Smith.

The **Blacksmith Shop** (#7) is one of the oldest buildings, dating from 1790; after the canal was opened in 1831, its business escalated, as the mules that towed the canal barges often needed new shoes.

Guard Lock 3 West (#3) and **Inclined Plane 4 West** (#9) are especially worth seeing if you're interested in the engineering aspect of the canal. The latter was recently named a National Historic Engineering Site. Imagine what it must have been like to move those heavy canal boats (weighing about 75 tons each) up this high vertical rise! You can learn more about the technical aspects of these operations and the history of the canal at the **Canal Museum** (#17).

The **Sawmill** (#10), **Gristmill** (#11), and **Stagecoach Inn and Tavern** (#12) are next. The sawmill is a re-creation (simulating those used before the Civil War), while the other two buildings are original, dating from the 1700s.

Though the 1760 **Miller House** (#13), the 1874 **Peter D. Smith House** (#14), and the late eighteenth century **Ironmaster's House** (#15) are not open to the public, you can still enjoy these originals from the outside, as you walk by them.

Take a quick look at the site of the **Andover Forge** (#16), now reduced to a grassy mound, before reaching the **Canal Museum** (#17), now the Museum of the Canal Society of New Jersey. Here you can see photographs of the boats and the men who drove them, as well as other items involving canal life. Note the model of the Morris Canal and its locks and inclined planes, which gives you a clear picture of its workings. Outside the museum you won't want to miss the lovely Perennial Garden, with its giant hibiscus, lavender, peonies, locust, and potted topiary junipers.

Continue walking along the water's edge, which will eventually lead to the re-created 400-year-old **Lenape Village** on its own separate island.

We now circle back through the village, on the inland route shown on the map. Among the attractions not to be missed before returning to your car is the delightful **Herb Garden** (#22), one of several little gardens scattered throughout the village. Here you'll find quite a collection of culinary, fragrant, and medicinal herbs (used to cure minor afflictions such as colds and sore throats). A formal knot edging encloses this pretty display.

16·
MILLBROOK
VILLAGE

Millbrook Village

*Exploring a
Nineteenth-Century Ghost Town*

❧ HOW TO GET THERE

Take I-80 to exit 4C, then Route 94 north for 9 miles to traffic light at Blairstown; turn left (as if to follow Route 521 north), then straight onto Route 602 north, through Blairstown; at stop sign (part-way up the hill) make a right and continue to follow Route 602 to Millbrook. The distance from the traffic light in Blairstown to Millbrook Village is 7.3 miles. The village is located at the junction of Old Mine Road and Route 602.

❧ INFORMATION

The grounds of Millbrook Village are open year-round, dawn to dusk; usually, the buildings are open on summer weekends and on the first full weekend in October, when the community celebrates "Millbrook Days," but phone first for confirmation. Telephone: 908-841-9531, or the Delaware Water Gap: 570-588-2451; Web site: www.millbrooknj.com.

❧ Ghost towns are mysterious and intriguing. As you walk through their silent streets, you might wonder what they once were like and why they were abandoned. Such a place is Millbrook Village, a tiny, remote, and difficult-to-find restored farm community set in a valley on a wooded hillside within the Delaware Water Gap National Recreation Area. This now quiet spot was, in the late nineteenth century, a thriving village with about twenty buildings and—at its height—some seventy-five inhabitants. Occasionally the village comes back to life, though only very briefly, when on given days in summer and early fall it opens its doors to the outside world. On those days you can catch a glimpse into the valley's village life during the late nineteenth and early twentieth centuries. But most of the time you are likely to have the place entirely to yourself, with only the sound of the wind blowing through the trees.

We first came upon Millbrook Village on a bleak, wintry day, when it was shut down tight and appeared quite abandoned, with just the atmosphere you would expect of a ghost town. Walking about, we noted the rustic structures with wood fences, the pretty country church, the gristmill along the rushing water. The dense forest and looming mountains of the Kittatinny Ridge behind the village added to our sense of isolation.

The origins of the village date to 1832, when Abram Garis built a gristmill along Van Campen Brook. As farmers brought their grain here (without having to make the arduous trip over the rugged mountains), others came to work at the mill and to provide services for the community. By the

1870s, Millbrook was a bustling (though tiny) commercial center, with a hotel, blacksmith shop and other stores, Methodist Church, school, and at least a dozen dwellings. Its fortunes changed, though, after a railroad line was built on the opposite side of Kittatinny Ridge, bypassing the village, which took business elsewhere; and with the general decrease in farming population at the turn of the century, Millbrook declined further, as did other villages in the valley. By the early 1900s, the gristmill had closed, along with most businesses in town (the blacksmith was the last to go, in the 1950s). By the time the Park Service took over, Millbrook had only a few occasional summer residents and had become a virtual ghost town.

Today the somewhat refurbished village includes at least six of the original buildings, along with other old buildings of the same era brought in from outside locations and some newer constructions built in a similar style. Despite these changes, the original village layout has been kept more or less intact, giving Millbrook its authenticity. Inside the buildings are period furnishings and objects relating to village life. During summer weekends and on "Mill Brook Days" in early fall, craft demonstrations by skilled artisans are offered to visitors; costumed guides and docents are also on hand to provide further historic insights.

Whether you prefer seeing Millbrook as a ghost town or as a tourist attraction is, of course, up to you. There are about twenty-five sites to visit, including an old cemetery; following are some of the main attractions.

After parking your car, stop at the **Spangenburg Cabin,** one of the few log cabins still in existence in the area. Lester Spangenburg, an early settler, dismantled a log cabin to build this house. Here you'll find literature about the community, lists of daily activities, and a self-guided walking tour.

The **Wagon Shop,** rebuilt in 1988 from the remains of an old barn, was where wagons, carts, and buggies were built and fixed. Near it is the carriage shed (also a new construction), which contains many kinds of wagons.

One of the original buildings of Millbrook is the **Trauger House,** named after its owner, a prosperous businessman.

The **Blacksmith Shop,** built near the site of the original one, was central to the village: here tools were repaired and sharpened, and such indispensable items as horseshoes were made. In season you might catch a blacksmith at work, perhaps demonstrating with dramatic flair how to shape a piece of iron in the flaming forge.

The **Cider Mill**, where cider, vinegar, or applejack were made, was another important part of village life. This building replaced the original on the same site. (When it's open you might see a demonstration of cider making.)

The **General Store** was vital to the community; here villagers could buy items not locally made or grown in exchange for farm products or handmade goods. Customers were able to pick from more than four hundred items, including medicines, groceries, hardware, and dry goods. The store also contained a small post office. The existing structure was brought here from another location in the valley (the old general store burned down).

The **Gristmill**, around which the village grew, stands out for its picturesque setting and lovely water views. The existing mill, erected by Millbrook volunteers in the late 1980s using felled timber (the original mill was another fire casualty), is still a work in progress; eventually its waterwheel is expected to work again, providing power to turn the grist stones in the building. Before leaving this site don't miss taking the short and scenic "race walk," starting just to the right of the entrance; the path circles back behind the village, offering great views along the way.

The charming **One-Room Schoolhouse** was originally the village church, dating from 1840. The "new" village church was built in 1860; the existing church is a faithful reconstruction dating from 1972.

Among the many other sites worth seeing—Millbrook Hotel, the smokehouse, drying house, woodworking shop, Van Campen Farmhouse and barn, and others—is the village cemetery, located on the hill above the school. On the old gravestones you can still make out the names of some of Millbrook's earliest residents. You might want to linger at this evocative spot.

❦ IN THE VICINITY

Van Bunschooten Museum, 1097 Route 23, Stillwater Township. Set amid 6.5 acres, this 1787 Dutch Colonial house with its period furnishings gives a good idea of the Dutch settlers' way of life in the eighteenth century. Telephone: 973-875-5335.

17·
HOPE

Hope

A Moravian Settlement

 HOW TO GET THERE

From Route 80 west, take exit 12 to Route 521 south, and follow signs for about 2 miles.

⚜ INFORMATION

While you can visit Hope year-round, it is especially inviting in spring and autumn—the fall colors of the surrounding countryside can be truly magnificent. You can take your own self-guided tour (a brochure with complete listings and map is available at the Inn at Millrace Pond, the former Moravian gristmill). Guided tours are also offered from April through November, on the first and second Saturday of the month. Telephone: 908-459-9177 or 459-4884.

⚜ The town of Hope, with its Moravian heritage, has an especially intriguing history and is still a vibrant community. Little has changed since its Moravian beginnings in the mid-eighteenth century, and the explorer can still visit many of the same buildings, as well as the gristmill and cemetery.

The Moravians were a pious, hard-working religious sect from Moravia and Bohemia in Central Europe. Their roots date to the fifteenth century, well before Martin Luther, when the followers of John Hus of Moravia (leader of a revolt against the Catholic Church) had to flee to the mountains; there they created their sect. Groups of Moravians arrived in America beginning around 1735 to escape persecution. In 1768, after moving to different locations, they were offered 1,000 acres by Samuel Green in western New Jersey, for which they paid one thousand pounds sterling.

A few years later the community was fully developed, becoming one of the first planned communities in America. It included a large, stone gristmill (at the foot of High Street—one of the town's earliest structures); the limestone *Gemeinhaus* (corner of Union and High Streets), which started as a community center, later serving as a church, a courthouse, and finally a bank; residences; a tavern; a school; a distillery; and numerous other structures. Some 150 people lived here—in log cabins, stone houses, and communal arrangements.

During the Revolutionary War, the Moravians, who were conscientious objectors, did not serve but provided nursing care for wounded American soldiers. A severe epidemic of smallpox virtually closed down the thriving community in 1799, reducing its population by half. The

Moravians who were left sold the community of Hope for $48,000 and moved west to Bethlehem, Pennsylvania. Hope then became a village of farmers—no industry came here, due to the town's remoteness and lack of transportation facilities. In 1973 it was entered into the State and National Register of Historic Places to preserve its historic integrity.

A walk through this uncommercial historic village is a treat for architecture buffs, too. Note some of the features typical of Moravian architecture: red brick window arches and chimneys, limestone window arches, economical use of cut stone, deeply pitched roofs, and two-story attics.

Although Hope is a small village within just a few blocks, there are more than thirty sites to see, all clearly indicated in the village brochure. In case you cannot see every one of them, here are some highlights not to be missed. Begin your circular walk at the foot of High Street, where you'll find the gristmill, now the Inn at Millrace Pond. Dating from 1769–70, the gristmill is the oldest building in the village; it was used during the Revolutionary War to grind grain for Washington's troops.

The **Moravian Distillery** (Millbrook Road), built in 1775, was the site of rye whiskey and beer production, with the brewmaster and his family occupying the second floor.

The oldest remaining stone residence (1775–76) is the quaint **Farm Manager's House and Barn** on Walnut Street. Note that the barn is one of two original Moravian barns to be found here, the other being Nicolaus Barn, on the corner of Cedar and Hickory Streets.

Look for the sites of two log cabins on Walnut Street once occupied by two early settlers in Hope, Peter Worbass (first manager of the community) and Samuel Green. It's presumed that the cellar of the present house was part of Worbass's 1769 cabin.

The old **Moravian Log Tavern** on Walnut Street is where George Washington apparently dined with his troops in 1782. In the mid-1800s a church was built here. The present building was restored in the 1950s as a community center.

The **Stephen Nicolaus House** on Hickory Street, built in 1775–76, was the second oldest stone house of the village. Note the original double herringbone doors and latches, a typical feature of Moravian architecture. The basement of this house became Hope's first public school in the early 1800s.

Around the corner on High Street are a 1780 **Moravian house;** the 1832 **Canal Era House,** now a conference center; and the site of **St. John's United Methodist Church,** built in 1832 after the Moravian era (the existing building dates from 1879).

Behind is the 1773 **Moravian Cemetery,** which contains sixty-two graves, all very simple and plain. On each rectangular stone slab you can read the name and birth and death dates and a number that corresponds to the list of burials in the Moravian Archives at Bethlehem. Those buried here all died between 1773 and 1808.

St. Luke's Episcopal Church on Hickory Street was built in 1832 of native limestone. Note its interior spiral staircase, which is said to have been based on a design by Sir Christopher Wren.

The **Gemeinhaus** on the corner of High Street and Route 519, dating from 1781, was certainly one of the most important structures in the early history of Hope. Here the Moravian community worshiped. Men and women used separate staircases that led to the church room on the second floor. On the first floor were the pastor's living quarters, as well as a small school for boys. Later, in 1824, the building was used as the county courthouse, then as an inn, and, since 1911, as a bank.

Next to the Gemeinhaus, farther down the road, are more Moravian houses dating from 1780–1800. Across the street was the Somge Sosters School, dating from 1803. The last structure built by the Moravians in Hope, it housed the colony's unmarried women, then became a girls' school, a florist shop, and finally an office building.

The **Long House,** near corner of High and Walnut streets, is an original Moravian stone structure dating from about 1777 (some parts were added later on). Over the years, it, too, has been used for many different things: confectionery stores, butcher shop, and post office. Today it contains shops, offices, and exhibition space. Right next to it is the **Hope Historical Society Museum,** a building that dates from the early 1800s and was probably the bridge toll house. The museum is open on weekends during the summer.

Finally, don't miss the so-called **Moravian Bridge** across High Street, a stone bridge actually built after the Moravians left, between 1810 and 1820.

18·
BELVIDERE

Belvidere

A Victorian Architectural Gem

❧ HOW TO GET THERE

Take Route 80 west through most of the state; go south on route 519, then south on route 618 and follow signs to Belvidere.

❧ INFORMATION

You can visit the town at any time of year or day, of course. If you would like a guided tour through some of the historic houses, check out the annual event (in September of each year) called "Victorian Days" on which certain private historic houses are open to the public. For further information, telephone the Warren County Historic Society (open on Sundays, from 2 to 4 P.M.), at 908-475-4246; Web site: www.belviderenj.com.

❧ Belvidere is aptly named. This scenic river town on the eastern shores of the Delaware is blessed with beautiful views. A small river, the Pequest, flows right through the heart of town, adding to the picturesque ambience. Yet Belvidere's visual appeal extends far beyond its natural setting: Belvidere is, in fact, an architectural gem boasting more than two hundred structures listed on the National Register.

Here, surrounding a spacious square park dotted with magnificent trees, are streets lined with historic mansions. Though most are from the Victorian era (the town is often referred to as "Victorian Belvidere"), there are fine examples from the colonial and other periods, too. Their variety is quite fascinating, including such features as turrets, columns, wrap-around porches, gingerbread, and other fanciful details. Shaded by beautiful old oaks, elms, and pines, most of these elegant buildings have been carefully preserved and are proudly maintained. (One definitely senses a pro-active community spirit here!) On prominent display in front of the square is the imposing nineteenth-century courthouse, a testament to Belvidere's enduring role as the county seat.

Like much of New Jersey, this area was once occupied by the Leni-Lenape, whose old village, Pesquase, is said to have been located here. As the Native Americans moved west across the Delaware, this early site evolved from strategic settlement with forts and stockades to farming community. William Penn was one of the first to purchase land here, in the early 1700s.

In 1769, Major Robert Hoops, who would eventually give Belvidere its name and be regarded as town founder, purchased land on both sides of the Pequest River from Penn. Hoops sold the south side parcel to Robert Morris, a prominent financier of the Revolution and signer of the Declaration of Independence, who in turn built a large plantation house for his daughter, Mary Croxall; one of the earliest of Belvidere's grand mansions, it is still standing, at 116 Greenwich Street. Garret Wall, a lawyer and later Governor of New Jersey, bought the Croxall property in 1825 and eventually subdivided the land into building lots, thus laying the foundation for the town.

Through the industrial era, Belvidere prospered with its mills powered by the Pequest River. As the town grew in stature (it became the county seat in 1824), more elaborately decorated houses sprang up, mostly on the square and surrounding streets just south of the Pequest. Today a visit to Belvidere is a must for anyone with a special interest in historic architecture. It's best to discover the town's heritage on foot, of course. Some of the buildings are accessible to the public on a regular basis; others are privately owned and can be visited only by special arrangement or through the "Victorian Days" house tours offered each year on the second or third weekend of September. But you are always free to explore on your own, perhaps by following the suggested route given below, in any order you like.

Park your car on Front Street, at the corner of Greenwich. Among the houses to note, as you walk south on Greenwich to Fourth Street, are the following:

#115: A circa 1880 Victorian, this structure, known as the Judge Morrow Law Office (it used to be located right near the courthouse), features molded window hoods and a heavily decorated vergeboard.

#116: This Georgian-style house (with a Daughters of the American Revolution historic plaque) from the 1780s is the aforementioned Croxall Mansion and is an important example of Belvidere's colonial period. Inside is an elegant winding staircase of polished walnut leading to bright, airy, spacious rooms. Privately owned, it is often included on historic house tours.

#220: This highly ornate Victorian, circa 1890, is well endowed with gingerbread decoration surrounding a beautiful round front window.

#300: A hard-to-miss Victorian, one of the largest and most elegant in town, it was built in 1880 by Judge William Morrow, who defended several county officials in the infamous "Ring Trials" of the 1870s. Note the octagonal bay wing, rounded window hoods, and porch.

At Fourth Street turn left and walk to **#142**, a handsome circa 1860 house with original clapboard exterior. Turn left on the next block, at Mansfield, a street with an eclectic collection of late Victorian houses, as well as some dating from the 1920s and 1930s. Note especially:

#424: It might surprise you to learn that this Tudor-style house actually came from a Sears Roebuck catalog in 1930. In fact, between 1908 and 1940, prospective home buyers would contact the company, which would then send them all the necessary supplies and plans. (Apparently some 450 such plans were built across the country from these catalogs.)

#410: This is a "pseudo-colonial," which was remodeled from its original Victorian style.

#314: Though it looks authentically Victorian, this house was built recently—in 1993.

#313: A simple Federal-style townhouse from c. 1845, this is now the home of the Museum of the Warren County Historical and Genealogical Society.

#302: A turn-of-the-century "Colonial Revival," this house is distinctive for, among other things, its Corinthian capitals.

The **Cummins Building**, on the corner of Mansfield and Second, is a fine example of Georgian architecture. Built in 1834 from limestone mined in a local quarry, it features an elegant entrance with classic, recessed columns.

On your right is Belvidere's inviting town square, a focal point of the town. Established in 1840, Garrett Wall Park was named after the town planner who donated this land to remain forever an open public space for walks, picnics, and other leisurely activities. From here you can enjoy nice town views on all four sides surrounding the square.

Leave the square on the south side and walk east (left) on Third Street to Knowlton. En route, note the following houses on Third:

#303: This 1840s house is a combination of Greek Revival (its facade), Victorian (porch pilaster corner boards, entrance), and Italianate (cornice brackets).

#404 and #406: Both are examples of Greek Revival, with such details as decorative brackets and pedimented window hoods and Ionic recessed columns.

#514: This 1897 Queen Anne is one of the grandest on Third Street. Note its turret, second-story porch, and oriel window.

#525: A gracious 1870s Italianate example with central gable, round arched window, ceiling-to-floor windows in front, and a charming carriage house, too.

#530: On the corner of Third and Knowlton, this terrific 1896 Queen Anne Victorian features a decorated wrap-around porch, stained glass sashes, corner tower, and hipped roof. Its interior is quite lavish, with antique wallpapers and furniture.

Turn left on Knowlton, walk one block, and turn left on Second. At **#301**, corner of Second and Hardwick, is the Blair Estate, now home of the Warren County Library. Built in 1865, it is a stuccoed structure with Italianate touches—an elaborate porch, overhanging eves, and molded window hoods.

The Warren County Courthouse dominates all other buildings on the street. Erected in 1827, this grand edifice remained unchanged until it was remodeled in 1959. On this site some highly publicized trials took place, especially in the nineteenth century, including the Carter-Parks murder trial in 1844 (with subsequent hanging), and the Ring Trials, involving fraud and embezzlement by local politicians. The view from the courthouse to the square and Garrett Wall Park is spectacular.

Turn right onto Mansfield Street and walk one block north to Front. On the way, note:

#228: This circa 1860 Victorian (a k a The Hilton House) is a grand Italianate mansion with ornate window hoods, a large decorative front porch, and molded and paneled front doors.

#101: Now the United National Bank, this beautiful structure dates from 1929, just before the Great Depression. Note the decorative relief just below the roofline.

On Front Street, don't miss:

#83: A T-shaped Victorian from the 1880s, with wrap-around porch and beveled-glass entrance.

#87: Also from the 1880s, this Italianate Victorian features a classic column porch and central gable peak.

#312–314: Note the fluted cast-iron columns on both houses.

#329: Dating from circa 1840, this house features a front entrance with sidelights and transom, molded door, and window trim.

You should now be near the spot where you parked your car. If you wish to explore further, we recommend walking (or driving) to the end of Prospect Street (walk east on Front Street for a couple of blocks, turn left onto Harwich, which becomes Prospect after you cross the Pequest River and Water Street). Here you will find the **Robert Hoops House**, home of the town founder. Now housing the Belvidere Rotary Club, this small one-and-a-half-story house dates from the 1760s and is considered among the town's oldest buildings.

✿ IN THE VICINITY

Oxford. Don't miss walking through the picturesque Oxford Furnace Village (a self-guided walking tour is available). Though most of the sites within the village are private property (and therefore can be enjoyed only on the outside), two are open to the public: the **Oxford Furnace** (dating from 1741) and **Shippen Manor Museum** (housed in a building from circa 1754; telephone: 908-453-4381). The Furnace, around which the village grew, today includes only a front building (called the "blow house") and the furnace structure itself. Shippen Manor, located at the corner of Belvidere and Washington Avenues, was the grand home of the original owners of the local iron works. Its many offerings include exhibits as well cultural and historical events during the year. Note the sweeping view of town from its lovely grounds.

19·
CLINTON

Clinton Red Mill

A Riverside Mill
Village and Quarry

❀ HOW TO GET THERE

The Red Mill Museum Village is located right in downtown Clinton, at 56 Main Street. From the New Jersey Turnpike, take exit 14 to I-78 west. At exit 15 (Clinton/Pittstown) follow signs to Clinton. Turn right onto West Main Street, then left at Clinton House. You'll find the Museum Village entrance about 50 yards away.

❀ INFORMATION

The Museum Village is open early April through early October, Tuesday through Saturday, 10 A.M. to 4 P.M., and Sundays, noon to 5 P.M. Closed on Mondays. Telephone: 908-735-4101; Web site: www.clintonnj.com.

❀   The Red Mill in the heart of historic Clinton is among the most photographed sites in New Jersey. And no wonder: set in idyllic splendor along a rushing waterfall on the banks of the Raritan River, it is a picture-postcard beauty, delightful in color and shape. To take in the full scene you can stand on the narrow bridge overlooking the falls or on the opposite shore near a lovely old stone building, once a mill itself. From here you often see ducks and geese swimming lazily in the tranquil waters just above the falls. Occasionally a few "tumble" over the waterfall's edge, landing below in an awkward splash—an amazing sight!

The historic mill is part of a ten-acre stretch nestled along the quiet river banked by fruit trees. Known as the Red Mill Museum Village, it is listed with the National Register of Historic Places. The village also includes towering limestone cliffs and quarry, and a dozen or so structures scattered about the grassy expanse—among them a blacksmith shop, a tiny schoolhouse, and a log cabin. Some are original, others are replicas, and all feature exhibits of one kind or another (we're told some 40,000 artifacts are on permanent or rotating display—from vintage dollhouses and toys to rocks and fossils of the region to Victorian household accessories). Unlike many tourist spots, this one has been kept as natural, uncommercial, and unfussy as possible, giving you the feeling of being in a genuine early nineteenth century rural village. This is a perfect place for children, too—in fact, you may well run into school groups on weekdays.

The Red Mill, built around 1810 to process wool, was originally a smaller structure, and perhaps not red at all. For the next one hundred years it changed hands many times over and was used in a surprising variety of ways: to process grains, graphite, and plaster; to produce peach baskets; to pump water and generate electricity for Clinton's street lamps. In the early twentieth century the mill was even grinding talc, one of its last operations, and as such was referred to as the "White Mill." Remnants of the equipment used for talc processing can still be seen in the building.

In the 1960s the mill was bought by local entrepreneurs who turned it into the Clinton Historical Museum. Soon after, the quarry behind it and its outbuildings were added to the property. The quarry had been founded by the Mulligan brothers in 1848 beneath the sheer limestone cliffs; they had burned the limestone and produced crushed stone. (This precious material had been used on railroad beds and on the many roadways being paved during the latter part of the nineteenth century.) The Mulligans had also helped to rebuild Clinton after a fire destroyed its Main Street in 1891.

The Red Mill Museum Village came together as additional structures were built or brought in from other locales. A popular tourist destination with many thousands of visitors each year, the village today offers special programs for school groups and the general public, including historic reenactments that take place on the vast lawn beneath the cliffs.

You can visit the village on your own, using the walking guide with map available in the entrance to the mill. Here you'll find many exhibits of interest (some permanent, others changing), from antique quilts to farm equipment and tools. But what we especially enjoyed was looking at the mill's waterwheel as it churned away, making its inimitable creaking sounds. And, of course, the view of the dramatic waterfall is irresistible.

Across from the mill and behind the Administration Building (where there are also changing exhibits) is the M. C. Mulligan & Sons Quarry Office. Dating from 1916, it is original to the site and stands in front of the dramatic cliffs. Surrounding it are several other structures connected with the quarry: the Screen House (1900), where the limestone rocks were sorted according to size; the Stone Crusher (1912); the Dynamite Shed (1916), which kept the dynamite used to dislodge the limestone from the cliffs (today it houses exhibits on subjects such as ice harvesting and fossils of the region); the lime kilns (1860), where limestone was burned to produce fertilizer for local farms; and Peg Leg's Shack, an original quarry worker's home dating from the early twentieth century.

The Blacksmith Shop (circa 1873) was also part of the quarry. It is a dark and mysterious-looking room, filled with tools of the trade. The Tenant House behind it (circa 1860) was originally home to two quarry worker families at a given time; today it appears as an old general store from the turn of the last century.

Perhaps our favorite of all the buildings is the Bunker Hill Schoolhouse. This is a must-see for children, who will be fascinated by the totally different school scene of the time. In this tiny one-room school, children of all grades were taught; girls and boys were separated across the aisle; unruly students had to don a dunce cap and sit in a corner (the dunce cap is still there); and the students had to use an outhouse. This tiny building with its characteristic school bell and steeple dates from about 1860 and was brought here from another township.

The log cabin behind it is a replica, based on the home of Daniel Morgan, a general during the Revolutionary War. Though cramped, we found it cozy, complete with a surprisingly short bed, a loft, a spinning wheel, and a welcoming fireplace for cooking. In front of the log cabin is an eighteenth-century-style herb garden featuring plants that were used at the time.

There are a few additional sites to see, all clearly identified and described. But be sure not to miss the romantic river views, as you make your way around the grounds.

After you leave the village, walk across the old iron bridge, where serious trout fishermen can be seen along its walking paths. In 1870 this picturesque bridge was put up to replace the original wooden bridge. On the opposite side of the river you'll find the other historic mill, now without a waterwheel. Constructed in 1836 on the site of an earlier mill that once ground wheat for George Washington's army, this old stone structure was built of limestone from the Mulligan Quarry. For many years it operated as a gristmill and later as a blacksmith shop and sausage factory. Today it houses the Hunterdon Museum of Art, featuring exhibits of contemporary art, and has also been placed on the State and National Historic Registers.

Don't leave Clinton without exploring its quaint Main Street, only a few blocks long. The town has carefully preserved its Victorian atmosphere and the architecture is wonderfully eclectic. Lining the streets you'll find a whole array of inviting antique shops and boutiques, as well as restaurants of various kinds, one or two along the river.

❦ IN THE VICINITY

Pittstown. The Alexandria Field Airport at 63 Airport Road is among the state's oldest air fields, dating from 1944. Though not particularly "historic" looking, it does include a number of antique airplanes, stored in hangars (thus not visible from the outside). Telephone: 908-735-0870.

20·
THE
PRALLSVILLE
MILLS

Prallsville Mills

A Tiny Historic Gem and Walk
along the Delaware and Raritan Canal

❧ HOW TO GET THERE

To *Prallsville Mills*

Take the New Jersey Turnpike to exit 14, then Route 78 west to exit 16, Route 31 south (toward Flemington), to Route 202 (west), toward Lambertville and the Delaware River; Route 29 north to Stockton. The Prallsville Mills are on the left-hand side of the road (going north), just after Stockton.

To *the* Covered *Bridge*

From the center of Stockton take Route 523 toward Sergeantville. Make a left on Covered Bridge Road. You'll come to the bridge before reaching Sergeantville.

❧ INFORMATION

The mills, operated by the Delaware River Mill Society at Stockton, are open when public events are held, which is quite often, as well as on occasional other days during the year; you can also call to make an appointment for a private tour. To check times, phone during office hours, Monday through Friday, 9 A.M. to 5 P.M. Of course you can enjoy the site from the outside and walk on the tow path at any time of the year, dawn–dusk. Telephone: 609-397-3586; Web site: www.njht.org/profiles/prallsville-mills.htm.

❧ One of our favorite spots along the historic Delaware and Raritan Canal is Prallsville Mills. This charming nineteenth-century mill complex, outside the pretty village of Stockton, is set right on the water, with easy access to an inviting shaded pathway just across a footbridge. This is an intimate place with just a handful of picturesque old buildings—a gristmill, grain silo, sawmill, linseed oil mill (the earliest, dating from 1794), and a few rustic sheds. Not surprisingly, this picture-perfect scene is also much photographed. Here you can experience history and nature all at once: first by walking around the historic site itself and enjoying it at least from the outside, if the buildings happen to be closed at the time; then by strolling along the path, which extends many miles on an abandoned railroad bed of the Belvidere and Delaware.

The D&R Canal was begun in 1830 and completed four years later; it was built during the pre-railroad era mainly to transport coal from Philadelphia to New York, to fuel its surging industrial economy. A largely Irish immigrant workforce manually dug the 44-mile-long Main Canal and its 22-mile feeder, an incredible feat considering the canal's width and depth. In the early years, boats and barges were pulled by mules and tow-paths were created; many of these towpaths were later used as railroad beds, and finally as recreational trails. The canal era ended in the late nineteenth century, with the domination of the railroad. After the D&R Canal finally closed in the 1930s, the state intervened; in the 1970s the entire length of the canal with its surrounding strip of land on both banks became a linear state park with lovely trails for walkers, joggers, cyclists, and even cross-country skiers.

Shaped roughly like a "V," the canal consists of two parts: the main canal (now reduced to 36 miles), extending from Bordentown and Trenton (on the Delaware) to New Brunswick (on the Raritan); and the feeder canal along the Delaware and Route 29, extending north from West Trenton almost to Milford. Both sections have more or less remained intact and still contain a number of historic structures, now listed on the National Register of Historic Places. Among these is, in fact, the site of Prallsville Mills.

Prallsville was named after John Prall, Jr., who in 1794 bought a wooden gristmill here, dating from the early 1700s. Replacing it with a more modern stone gristmill, the enterprising Prall added a sawmill and other structures, started a stone quarry, operated two fisheries, and transformed his tiny community into a viable commercial center.

The existing gristmill dates from 1877 (the original one was badly damaged in a fire) and operated through the 1950s. The state purchased Prallsville Mills in 1973, declared it a Historic Site, and soon made it a part of the Delaware and Raritan Canal State Park. The abandoned rail bed that passes through the mill was later converted into the picturesque trail you see today; and the Delaware River Mill Society, a group of local preservationists, has since undertaken some building restoration—with more to follow. The society also sponsors arts and environmental events that take place right on the premises: art exhibits (in the Linseed Oil mill), as well as concerts, antique shows, and auctions.

Despite these many activities, the site is refreshingly uncommercial and untouristy. The buildings are open on a somewhat sporadic basis; if you wish to visit them inside (usually by guided tour), phone ahead (see above) and plan your trip accordingly, so as not to be disappointed. But even on an "off" day, you are free to walk around the site and learn a little something about its history from information signs posted in front of the buildings. And, of course, you can take your canal walk at any time of the year, savoring the views of the Delaware River beyond and its tiny islands. If you're feeling particularly energetic, we recommend the scenic 3-mile walk north to **Bull's Island Natural Area**, a small wooded island popular with hikers and campers.

❧ IN THE VICINITY

Two other nearby historic sites that are worth a stop are the village of Stockton and an old covered bridge. Stockton, a sleepy ferry town dating to the early eighteenth century, is probably best known today as the site of the **Stockton Inn**, immortalized by the Rodgers and Hart show song containing the words "There's a small hotel with a wishing well." The hotel in question—formerly the Colligan's Stockton Inn, dating to 1710—is still there, with its famous wishing well, too. Be sure to take a walk through the village, which has retained much of its old-fashioned charm.

The second spot not to be missed is **Green Sergeant's Bridge**, a few miles away, just outside Sergeantsville. This covered bridge, the only existing one in the state, crosses a rushing brook along a winding road quite off the beaten path. Dating to 1872, it was restructured in 1961 and is among the most picturesque structures we have seen in the region.

21·
PRINCETON
CEMETERY

Aaron Burr Gravestone at Princeton Cemetery

*Burial Site of Presidents
and Other Notables*

❧ HOW TO GET THERE

Take the New Jersey Turnpike to exit 9; go Route 1 south, then Washington Road into Princeton. Turn left onto Nassau Street. At Witherspoon Street turn right. You'll see the cemetery on the corner of Witherspoon and Wiggins; turn right on Wiggins, then left onto Greenwood Avenue, to the entrance at the end.

❧ INFORMATION

You can visit the cemetery on your own (pick up a map at the superintendent's house on the cemetery grounds) or by guided tour. Open daily, year-round. For information or to make arrangements for a tour, call 609-924-1369.

❧ Princeton is no doubt best known to outsiders for its prestigious university; but it is also an important historic town with quite a number of interesting sites for visitors. One of our favorites is the Princeton Cemetery, a leafy and quiet corner property with almost 19 acres to wander through and explore.

The cemetery has sometimes been called the "Westminster Abbey of the United States," and for good reason: Here are the graves of distinguished figures in politics, government, academia, and the arts, a veritable "who's who." The list is quite impressive, combining public as well as less-known figures, from university presidents to signers of the Declaration of Independence; from poets and musicians to mathematicians and scholars. Even a United States president is buried here—Grover Cleveland, who lived in Princeton from 1897 to 1908—as is a vice president, Aaron Burr. Though names like Bayard, Terhune, Leonard, and Stockton might not mean much to most visitors, these notable families are well represented here as part of the town's rich historical legacy.

Established in 1757, the cemetery is the second-oldest burial ground in town, after the Quaker cemetery dating from about 1724. But, unlike the Quakers' burial ground whose earliest graves were left unmarked (a Quaker custom of the time), the names here are clearly indicated. The oldest part of the cemetery, formerly called the Old Graveyard, lies along the intersection of Wiggins and Witherspoon streets. This one-acre parcel was first acquired by the College of New Jersey (now Princeton University) soon after its seventy students had been moved from Newark to the just completed Nassau Hall, which is still the university's most prominent building. The land was eventually taken over by the Nassau Presbyterian Church; the cemetery gradually expanded, first with the addition of the adjacent Wiggins Farm, then with other parcels. With its final assimilation of 8 acres bequeathed by Moses Taylor Pyne in 1919, the cemetery reached its present size. Few grave sites are still available today, though a former mayor of Princeton, Barbara Sigmund, was buried here as recently as 1990.

Just beyond the entrance to the graveyard you'll find a cemetery map with all the information you'll need, including history, notable grave markers, and who is buried where. (Note that though the numberings on the map may seem somewhat random in their order, everything is clearly documented.) Begin at the flagpole, and follow the path slightly to your left. One of the first graves you will come to is that of William H. Hahn, Jr. (#16); if graves can be witty, this one is, bearing the epigraph "I told you I was sick." Continue on the pathway, where you'll find quite a collection of graves: among others, those of a Confederate brigadier general, a founder of the Daughters of the American Revolution, as well as several notable university professors. Don't miss two important markers: the first, to President Grover Cleveland (#9), who had two terms in office, from 1885 to 1889 and from 1893 to 1897 (his birthday, on March 18, is celebrated here each year with an impressive wreath-laying ceremony); and the second, to the much-honored writer John (Henry) O'Hara (#33), with its epitaph, "Better than anyone else he told the truth about his time. He wrote honestly and well."

By far, the most visited site is the Presidents' Plot in a section along Wiggins Street, where the markers of eleven of the fifteen former presidents of the college and university can be found. (The missing four are Jonathan Dickinson, president of the college in 1747; Samuel Finley; Francis Landey Patton; and Woodrow Wilson.) Here, under lovely old trees, are the monuments of such illustrious names as Aaron Burr, Sr. (his is the oldest grave in the cemetery); his son Aaron Burr, Jr., the vice president of the United States, who engaged Alexander Hamilton in that infamous duel in Weehawken (see walk 2); and Jonathan Edwards, noted clergyman as well as university president. Be sure to find, in addition, the nearby grave of George H. Gallup, creator of the famous Gallup Poll.

Not far from the Presidents' Plot is the Old Graveyard along Witherspoon Street. Here you can see the names of some of the earliest European families, including that of Margaret Leonard, the first European child born in Princeton (her grave is the second oldest in the cemetery) and Thomas Wiggins, a physician who bequeathed a significant amount of land to the cemetery. Behind his grave is a stately old elm tree, one of the finest in the entire graveyard, which now encircles several tombs.

Find your way back to the flagpole, from where you can explore the other half of the cemetery. Though not as old, it nevertheless contains some important markers as well as lovely trees, and is definitely worth a visit. Don't miss the grave of Sylvia Beach (#4), located on the path to the right beyond the office. The founder of Shakespeare & Company, she courageously published (in Paris, in 1922) James Joyce's *Ulysses,* a work that many contemporaries found obscene.

✿ IN THE VICINITY

Princeton University Campus, Nassau Street. A trip to Princeton must include a visit to the university's beautiful campus with its Gothic and modern buildings, extraordinary outdoor sculptures and first-rate museum, charming gardens, great trees, and its sense of the gracious past. At its center is the noted Nassau Hall, a Georgian stone structure dating from 1756; it served as a hospital for troops during the Revolutionary War and was, in 1783, the site of the drafting of the Constitution when Princeton was the nation's capital. Today it serves as an administrative building for the University. Walk around the campus on your own, or take a guided tour from MacLean House, offered regularly at no cost. Telephone: 609-258-3603.

Morven Museum and Garden, 55 Stockton Street, Princeton. Morven, formerly the governor's mansion (and originally the home of Richard Stockton, a signer of the Declaration of Independence), is a gracious Georgian mansion open to public tours on Wednesdays. (Phone for their schedule.) Telephone: 609-683-4495.

Drumthwacket (1835), 354 Stockton Street, Princeton. Drumthwacket (its rather unusual sounding name is Celtic for "wooded hill"), the present governor's mansion, is open to the public via guided tour on Wednesdays, for two hours. This elegant, recently refurbished Greek Revival house, reminiscent of plantation houses down south with its Ionic columns and gracious veranda, was built in 1835 by Charles Olsen, who had spent several years in New Orleans. Inside are historic paintings, period furnishings, silverware (from the battleship USS *Jersey*), and porcelains. Outside you can wander around the formal terraced gardens. Telephone: 609-683-0057.

For additional sites in the Princeton area, see walk 22.

22·
PRINCETON
BATTLEFIELD
STATE PARK

Princeton Battlefield

Scenes from the
Revolutionary War

❧ HOW TO GET THERE

From downtown Princeton go south on Nassau Street and turn left at Mercer Street. The park entrance is located on the left, at 500 Mercer Street, about 1.5 miles south from the center of town.

❧ INFORMATION

The park is open from dawn to dusk daily, year-round. Clarke House is open Wednesday through Saturday, 10 A.M. to noon, and 1–4 P.M.; Sunday, 1–4 P.M. Free. Telephone: 609-921-0074.

❧ Princeton Battlefield Park is not only an inviting place for a walk, but also an important historic site in its own right. Its 85 acres, situated on both sides of Mercer Road, include a vast field, a picturesque eighteenth-century house, and a colonnade and grave site. On what is today a peaceful spot with picturesque country views, a fierce battle once took place, one that marked a turning point in the Revolutionary War. A reenactment of the battle takes place in January.

Princeton played a pivotal role in that war. Strategically located on the main road between the Raritan and Delaware rivers, it was one of several towns occupied by the British troops. During the summer and fall of 1776 the Americans had suffered a series of defeats, and it seemed more than likely that the British would prevail. The situation began to shift when Washington successfully attacked the Hessian garrison in nearby Trenton in December 1776. In response, the British, under Lieutenant General Charles Cornwallis, fortified Princeton with more troops and planned an early, surprise attack for the morning of January 3, 1777.

In preparation, Cornwallis and most of his troops moved stealthily toward nearby Assunpink Creek (leaving some 1,200 men in Princeton), where they expected to find the American troops; but, unbeknownst to them, Washington and his men slipped away in the middle of the night, hours before the planned attack, wrapping the horses' hoofs into cloth to muffle their sounds, leaving only a few men behind as decoys. The Americans reached Princeton before dawn. The Battle of Princeton actually began in Thomas Clarke's orchard, when General Hugh Mercer's force attacked two British regiments. Though it was a very bloody battle with many casualties on both sides (including Mercer himself, who was bayoneted and died nine days later), the Americans ultimately prevailed, forcing the British to retreat to New Brunswick. The victory at Princeton proved to be a turning point in the war, ending any question of British domination.

Today you can walk around the site of the battle—a wide-open field with no set paths—and roam at will while imagining the events that took place here more than 250 years ago. Aside from the inviting allée of evergreens at the entrance, there are few trees in the park, so you can see the surrounding countryside.

On the park premises you'll also find the Thomas Clarke House (c. 1772), now the Princeton Battlefield State Park Museum. Here you can pick up brochures and information. Thomas Clarke was a Quaker farmer who lived a quiet life on his 200 acres on the edge of Princeton village, when history struck right on his property. After the battle, his house was used as a temporary hospital for wounded soldiers. Here General Mercer was cared for by Dr. Benjamin Rush (signer of the Declaration of Independence). The farm includes the original frame house, a carriage barn, and smokehouse. In an enlarged wing are exhibits relating to the Battle of Princeton and the war in general. Among the many items on display is the scarlet uniform of the Hessian commander who was killed at the Battle of Trenton.

Across the street is the Ionic colonnade and grave site. The four-columned colonnade, once the facade of an elegant Philadelphia home, was brought here in 1959 to mark the entrance to the common grave of British and American soldiers who died in battle. As the plaque behind the memorial reads, "Near here lie buried the American and British soldiers who fell in the Battle of Princeton, January 3rd, 1777."

If you're interested in pursuing yet another nearby Revolutionary War site, find the Princeton Battle Monument, situated on the corner of Stockton (Route 206) and Nassau Streets. Designed by the notable sculptor Frederick MacMonnies in the early 1920s, it depicts the unmistakable figure of George Washington in battle.

✄ IN THE VICINITY

Don't miss a walk or guided tour around the **Princeton University campus**, including a stop at historic Nassau Hall, built in 1756. Telephone: 609-258-3603. Also see walk 21.

Princeton has many additional historic sites, including the following:

Bainbridge House, 158 Nassau Street. Today the Historical Society's headquarters, this is a well-preserved example of Georgian architecture (1766), with an interesting history.

Maclean House, Princeton University campus. Built in 1756 for college presidents, this building was home to many illustrious figures.

Einstein House, 112 Mercer Street. Here in this c. 1840 house, the world-famous scientist lived from 1935 to 1955 while working at the Institute for Advanced Study. It is now a private residence. At the corner of Bayard Lane and Nassau Street, near the front of Borough Hall, you will find a newly erected memorial statue of Einstein engraved with a brief biography and famous quotations.

Paul Robeson's Birthplace, 110 Witherspoon Street. In this c. 1870 house, the noted singer, actor, and political activist lived for the first few years of his life. He was the son of the Reverend William Robeson of the nearby Witherspoon Presbyterian Church (1840s), a site of the Underground Railroad and other antislavery activities (124 Witherspoon Street).

23·
THE DELAWARE
AND RARITAN
CANAL

Early canal travel

A Towpath and Rail Trail Loop
from Kingston to Rocky Hill

❀ HOW TO GET THERE

From I-287, exit 17, past Bridgewater, take Route 206 south into Princeton, then left (north) onto Route 27 (Nassau Street) to Kingston. The Kingston Branch Loop Trail is located just north of Princeton's Lake Carnegie off Route 27. Park at the John Fleemer Preserve.

❀ INFORMATION

The trail is open daily, dawn to dusk, year-round. For general information call the Delaware and Raritan Canal State Park office: 732-873-3050. Telephone for information on Rockingham (located at 82 Laurel Avenue in Kingston): 609-683-7132. The house is open Wednesday through Saturday, 10 A.M. to noon and 1–4 P.M., and Sunday, 1 to 4 P.M.

❀ The Delaware and Raritan Canal offers some of New Jersey's most picturesque vistas, with miles of leafy waterside pathways to explore on foot (or bike); the fact that it is also among the state's most important historic landmarks makes a walk along its shores all the more rewarding. Not only are there water views at every turn, but also remnants of the canal era—quaint river villages, wooden bridges and locks, bridge-tender houses, and cobblestone spillways. Along parts of the canal are yet other signs of the past: the old rail beds where trains once ran, now converted to rail trails.

Though the D&R covers a large area—the main section now extends for 36 miles (of the original 44), and the feeder canal about 22 miles—the walk described below covers only about four miles of it, just enough to give you a taste of one of the many picturesque parts of the canal, and perhaps the incentive to see more. Earlier (see "The Prallsville Mills," walk 20, for a brief history of the canal) we discuss a site on the western section of the canal, along the Delaware; here instead, we focus on a section of the eastern part of the V-shaped D&R, along the Millstone River, a tributary of the Raritan River. This is a highly scenic loop that follows the route of a narrow rail corridor one way, crosses the canal over a small wooden bridge, then circles back on the canal towpath; it is varied, too, including, among other things, a nineteenth-century quarry and nearby manor house where George Washington wrote his famous speech, "A Farewell to the Troops" (and no doubt slept there, too!)

The Delaware and Raritan Canal was crucial to the state's economy, as it provided a key water route for transportation of goods between New York and Philadelphia. In its heyday in the 1860s and 1870s the boats on the D&R carried not only coal from Pennsylvania, but also grain, fertilizer, and other products; in fact, in the banner year of 1871 more cargo went through the channels of the D&R than in any single year on the better known and more celebrated Erie Canal.

But the D&R transported more than products. In fact, the company offered a "packet" or passenger service, for those who wished to travel across the state while enjoying the scenery along the canal. According to a chronicler of the time, these passengers included "ladies in crinolines holding gayly colored parasols to protect them from the sun . . . attended by gentlemen in high silk hats. Delightful the trip must have been during the day, but not at night, for then, according to Harriet Beecher Stowe . . . the passengers were packed like sardines into the small cabins with narrow berths rising in tiers one above the other." Though the trip was undoubtedly a pleasurable experience on many levels, it's understandable that most travelers ultimately preferred crossing New Jersey via the more rapid railroad.

One can only envision the assortment of boats that went up and down the canal—from coal barges, canal boats, tugs, sloops, even gunboats (during the Civil War) to the elegant white yachts that sailed on the canal at the turn of the century, carrying ladies and gentlemen on their way to and from southern waters during their seasonal voyages. Though the competition from the railroads sealed the fate of the D&R, it still continued operations throughout the first third of the twentieth century, until the state took over in 1934. In contrast to its early and bustling life, the canal today is a quiet place, where you can walk in peace and reflect on what it was like here a long time ago.

We especially like the following 4-mile loop because you don't need to retrace your steps. (Of course, another option is simply to do an "out and back" linear walk, which gives you more flexibility in terms of time.) After you've left your car, walk north through a tunnel under Route 27. You have a choice either to take the canal towpath (on your left) or the old railroad bed trail (right), knowing that in any case you'll experience them both if you do the loop. The paths are flat, with a fine stone dust surface that is very pleasant underfoot. You'll find they are nicely shaded with a variety of trees—sycamores, black locusts, oaks, among others; but back in the 1800s there was virtually no shade along the canal, as trees were cut so that mules and boats could pass easily.

On the canal towpath you'll catch sight of the Millstone River now and again, as it winds around, running more or less parallel to the canal. (It's a popular place for canoes.) Look for mallard ducks, herons, and cormorants in the tranquil canal waters.

Regardless of which way you go, you'll come to the turnaround point at a wooden bridge near the nineteenth-century village of Rocky Hill. If possible, take the time to explore this quaint little town, which in the old days had a gristmill, sawmill, taverns, and stores.

The path along the rail trail—once a spur of the Camden and Amboy Railway, built in 1864—goes by a surprisingly large quarry situated on a hillside. Begun in the 1860s and still functioning today, the quarry was one of the main reasons that the railroad came here in the first place. (This might be the only "noisy" part of the walk.) It yielded the trap rock used to pave many city streets in New Jersey and New York, some of which you may well have walked on.

Rockingham State Historic Site, which adjoins the path nearby, is your next stop. Originally located near Rocky Hill, it was moved a short distance to its present site in Kingston, to make way for the expanding quarry. This was Washington's final wartime headquarters. It was here that he wrote his famous "Farewell Orders to the Armies of the United States," which he delivered on November 2, 1783, after the Treaty of Peace marking the end of the war. He had leased the house from the widow of Judge Berrien, a prominent local jurist. Having composed his address in the upstairs chamber, Washington read it to his assembled staff from the balcony of the house. After bidding farewell to his troops, he made his long journey back to Virginia. The house remained in the Berrien family until the early nineteenth century, was later leased to the Rocky Hill Quarry Company (to house its laborers), and finally was designated a historic site. It now includes the mansion, a children's museum, and gardens, including a re-created eighteenth-century kitchen garden with herbs used at the time.

Also in Kingston, along Route 27, you'll find lock #8 (of the many in the D&R), the lock tender's house and station, and the old mill.

❧ IN THE VICINITY

Just a few miles north of Rocky Hill is the little village of **Griggstown**, filled with historic sites relating to the canal. (You can drive there from the parking lot at Kingston, either on Canal Road or on River Road, which is also Route 533.) This old community predates the canal era by centuries, as it was farmed by the Lenape Indians first, then the Dutch and the English. It included a gristmill, sampling mill (for local copper ore), a blacksmith, and a few stores. When the canal opened in 1834, Griggstown built two canal houses at the lock and a third at the bridge tender's place. Many of the original eighteenth- and nineteenth-century buildings still exist, making this a very special spot. Don't miss the Mule Tenders Barracks Museum at 4 Griggstown Causeway, right on the water; it will give you the full story. Telephone: 732-877-3050.

Another village worth exploring is **Blackwells Mills**, just north of Griggstown, on the same side of the canal. Here, too, are vintage buildings from the canal era: the bridgetender's house, mill site, and charming wooden bridge are among them. The canal house offers special events.

Other nearby sites of interest:

Buccleuch Mansion, Easton Avenue, New Brunswick. Once occupied by British troops, this 1739 Georgian mansion is furnished with Victorian antiques, folk art, and scenic wallpaper. And, yes, George Washington did sleep here! Limited visiting hours (call to check), but the surrounding park and gardens are open on a regular basis. Telephone: 732-745-5094.

The Meadows Foundation, Inc., 1289 Easton Avenue, Somerset. In six historic buildings, the foundation displays Delaware and Raritan Canal memorabilia and hosts events. Telephone: 732-828-7418.

The Old Millstone Forge Museum, North River Street, Millstone. This special museum is housed in one of the oldest continuously operating blacksmith shops in the nation. Featured is a fascinating collection of eighteenth-century blacksmith tools. Telephone: 732-873-2803.

24·
WASHINGTON CROSSING STATE PARK

Washington Crossing State Park

A Ferry Landing and Historical Center from the Revolutionary War

❧ HOW TO GET THERE

Take New Jersey Turnpike to exit 7A, then Route 195 west to Route 295 north (which becomes Route 95). Exit 1 will take you to Route 29. Go north; the entrance to the park is on your right, about one half mile from the intersection of Routes 29 and Route 546. Follow signs to Visitor Center.

❧ INFORMATION

The park is open during daylight hours throughout the year, but the Visitor Center is only open Wednesday through Sunday from 9 A.M. to 4:30 P.M. Be sure to pick up a self-guiding map. (Keep in mind that there is also a Crossing site on the Pennsylvania side of the river.) For information, telephone: 609-737-0623 or 609-737-9303; Web site: www.state.nj.us/dep/forestry/parknj/divhom.htm.

❧ This rather grand site is where the Continental Army under General George Washington landed after that famous Delaware nighttime crossing on Christmas night in 1776, a turning point of the Revolutionary War. It is a scenic 1,399-acre setting, with rolling hills and magnificent river views, offering both great hiking terrain and fully documented historic material. Walkers and history buffs alike will be satisfied by this outing: you'll find an interpretive center, the 1740 Johnson Ferry House, and a reproduction of a boat used by the troops. You can even climb up the banks of the river where the Continental Army made its way in the dead of night. There are also an arboretum, a nature center, and trails for hiking, camping, and fishing.

The famous event that is celebrated here (immortalized in the painting by Emmanuel Leutze and reproduced in most American history textbooks) is surely one of the most familiar events of the Revolution. Washington's brilliant strategy and derring-do combined to create the legendary event. It was here that the general and his troops crossed an ice-packed, wide, and swiftly moving Delaware River on a stormy night, surprising the British and their Hessian mercenaries on Christmas Day, and reversing the fortunes of the Continental cause. Though you won't be crossing the river itself to re-create this historic moment, there is a lot to see at the park, and you will be able to bring to life a sense of the past and the magnitude of the event.

In the autumn of 1776 the fortunes of the Continental Army were at a low point, with one defeat after another, and a long, bitter retreat from

Fort Lee on the banks of the Hudson to Pennsylvania. "Between you and me," wrote Washington to his brother, "I think our affairs are in a very bad condition." The British had settled in at Trenton (about 9 miles from here) for the winter. The Americans under Washington were camped in Pennsylvania, just across the Delaware (near what is New Hope today). The general's objective was to prevent the British from reaching Philadelphia.

The Continental Army was in great need of a victory, both to encourage new enlistees and Washington's own demoralized troops, and to reverse the direction the war had taken. On December 23, Washington wrote to Colonel Joseph Reed: "Christmas-day at night, one hour before day is the time fixed upon for our attempt on Trenton," and by 6 P.M. he and 2,400 men, with their horses and eighteen cannons, began the crossing in ferryboats. Due to "obstructions of ice in the river" they did not get across until two o'clock in the morning, under "a constant fall of snow with some rain." Another officer, Henry Knox, wrote, "The night was cold and stormy; it hailed with great violence." Material at the Visitor Center will tell you much more about this incredibly difficult crossing. Among the details you will learn is that the troops took with them three days' worth of cooked rations, blankets, and forty rounds of ammunition per soldier; that their bloody feet left tracks in the snow; and that their password was "Victory or Death."

At the same time, one thousand American militia were given orders to cross the river further south opposite Trenton and seize the bridge over a small river at the lower end of town, thus cutting off the enemy's possible retreat from Washington's attack.

On the arrival of the ferries, local people rushed to help the soldiers disembark. By the time everyone was unloaded and had reached Trenton it was daylight. But the surprised Hessians were caught unsuspecting. "The hurry, fright, and confusion of the enemy" led to an American victory and enabled the Continental Army to move on. Nine hundred and eighteen Hessians were captured, and the Americans lost two officers. Washington returned a few days later for a second successful battle at Trenton, and enjoyed a victory in Princeton the next day.

The 2.5-mile walk (almost completely flat) that the self-guided trail suggests begins at the first historic marker, where the troops landed. You will continue east, past a scenic overlook of the river, to the Johnson Ferry

House. This 1740 building was a guest tavern and the original spot from which ferries operated, and it was here that Washington and his officers were sheltered after their crossing and drew up their plans for the attack on Trenton. You can visit the interior of the house.

Not far away is the large stone barn, which was where the family living in the Ferry House resided. There are historic displays inside. Follow the path to the pedestrian bridge, where you'll see a reproduction of the ferryboat, typical of those used in the crossing. If you walk east along Continental Lane you'll follow the route Washington's army took toward Trenton. You will come to the Visitor Center on this pathway, and be sure to see the uniforms in the amazing Swan Collection of Revolutionary War artifacts. (Some visitors may prefer to begin their walk here.)

There is much, much more to be seen at Washington Crossing State Park; this is a very brief description, designed to whet your appetite for Revolutionary history. Unlike the battlefields we have visited elsewhere in this book, this site is not the scene of carnage and strategy, but of a brilliant tactical maneuver undertaken by a general and his woebegone army in the dead of winter.

✼ IN THE VICINITY

Howell Living Farm, in Titusville, on Valley Road, off Route 29. This 1900–10 house and farm has no modern equipment and invites visitors to join in field and barn programs in the style of a century ago. Telephone: 609-737-3299.

25·
MONMOUTH BATTLEFIELD STATE PARK

Monmouth Battlefield

*Walking through
Revolutionary War History*

❧ HOW TO GET THERE

Take the Garden State Parkway to exit 123 to Route 9 south. Go 15 miles to business Route 33 west. The battlefield park is 1.5 miles on your right.

❧ INFORMATION

Monmouth Battlefield State Park is a National Historic Landmark. The park center is open every day from 9 A.M. to 4 P.M., while the grounds are open to visitors longer hours, on a seasonal schedule. We recommend that you visit the center for an overview before you set out, and that you pick up a self-guiding map there. There are many events here, including tours and, on the fourth weekend in June every year, a reenactment of the battle. Telephone: 732-462-9616; Web site: www.njparksandforests.org.

❧ Monmouth Battlefield was an important turning point for the Continental Army in the Revolutionary War. It marked the first time the colonials fought the British army to a standoff in an open field. For two days in June 1778, one of the longest and largest battles of the war was fought here on the sloping hills and fields of Monmouth County. Many of the most important generals in the Continental Army took part in this battle.

The British Army, under the command of General Sir Henry Clinton, was marching from Philadelphia through New Jersey toward New York City in a long, snaking column that sometimes stretched for eight to ten miles. The Continental Army under General George Washington left Valley Forge and moved toward the massive British troop line that numbered some 20,000 men. On the morning of June 28 the two groups met: George Washington's 8,500 men were camped about four miles west of Englishtown. General Charles Lee—for whom this battle would become a personal nightmare—was ordered by Washington to take 5,000 troops and to attack the rear of the British Army as it moved across Monmouth. The heat was intense; temperatures were close to 100 degrees during the day of the battle.

General Lee encircled the British rear guard and then, under fire from the much larger British forces, began a retreat across Rhea Farm (part of today's walk). The American troops were guided to this location by Lieutenant Colonel David Rhea, who was born on a nearby farm and knew the terrain. But Lee's retreat was intercepted by General Washington, who ordered him to stay with the battle and wait for more troops to defend him. Washington was furious with Lee's decision, reportedly demanding, "I desire to know, sir, what is the reason, whence arises this disorder and confusion!" Reports tell us that Washington called Lee a "damned poltroon" and swore at the unfortunate officer "till the leaves shook on the trees." Lafayette was said to remember the incident all his life. (The affair concluded with a court martial and ended Lee's career.)

The British Army pushed its way across the fields nonetheless, coming to the dividing line of Spotswood South Brook. (You'll find two wooden bridges across this small brook today.) After bloody clashes at the wood and the hedgerows just beyond, the Americans eventually occupied a hill above the British troops called Perine Farm Hill; here they set up a line of ten guns. The British were unable to outflank the Continental Army and withdrew when they found General Lafayette's troops awaiting them on another side.

The skirmishes continued for much of the day until General Nathaniel Greene brought in a brigade of Virginians and four guns to the top of Combs Hill, thereby trapping the British troops between two hills, and forcing them to withdraw.

As the British regrouped, Washington counterattacked. Two battalions of Continental light infantry advanced along Spotswood North Brook, while General Anthony Wayne led three small regiments to attack the withdrawing enemy. Wayne's men were forced to shelter in the parsonage and orchard of Parsonage Farm (part of our walk). After Washington moved fresh troops and continued the assault, the British, having three times the casualties of the Continental Army, decided to quit the field. They were a defeated army, and they departed under cover of darkness that night. It was the last major battle of the north and is regarded as both a political and tactical triumph for the Continental Army. American scholars have often debated whether Washington could have decisively ended the war at Monmouth by blocking that retreat.

For the Americans, the battle created new enthusiasm, as well as new heroes and one heroine, in particular eighteen-year-old Molly Pitcher, who followed her husband John Hays into the battle. When the temperature soared on the battlefield, Molly Pitcher grabbed an artillery bucket and began bringing water to the soldiers and nursed the injured. She even dragged a wounded soldier to safety. When her husband was shot at his cannon, she spent the rest of the day loading the gun while under heavy fire. After the battle, Washington personally thanked her and issued her a warrant as a noncommissioned officer.

A complete walk around the site could take many, many hours, as there are some twenty-five miles of trails. But any part of the walk is both historically interesting and attractive. With map in hand you can reconstruct the events of these two important days in Revolutionary War history. We recommend the excellent displays in the Visitor Center, which will create for you a visual sense of what the army, armaments, and generals really looked like. You can choose to do the Combs Hill to the Hedgerow and Parsonage walk, with a self-guiding map. Or you can see some of the major sites with the help of the map in the "The Battle of Monmouth" flyer.

❧ IN THE VICINITY

There are several interesting buildings of historical note nearby. On the battlefield itself is **Craig House**, which was built in 1746–47 and is open to the public. Visit **Old Tennent Church** (1751) adjacent to the battlefield. There is also the Monmouth County Historical Association Museum at 70 Court Street in Freehold. Telephone: 732-462-1466.

26·
GEORGIAN
COURT COLLEGE

Georgian Court College

*The Robber Baron's Estate and
the Glories of Excess and Elegance*

❦ HOW TO GET THERE

Take the Garden State Parkway (from the north) to exit 91. The second traffic light is at County Line Road, which you should take for approximately 5 miles to Route 9. Take Route 9 south (left turn) and continue to Ninth Street. Turn right and proceed through the Forest Avenue intersection to Lakewood Avenue. Entrance to the college is on your right.

❦ INFORMATION

Georgian Court College can be visited during daylight hours. Be sure to check in at the entrance gate. Telephone: 908-364-2200 or 800-458-8422; Web site: www.georgiancourt.edu.

❦ Georgian Court College is a remarkable place to visit. Declared a National Historic Site in 1978, the campus was designed to replicate an English country estate of the Georgian era by George Jay Gould, the son of the railroad magnate and robber baron, Jay Gould, and a major industrialist as well. And what a sight it still is! Excess and elegance go together in these palatial grounds, filled with sculptures, fountains, landscaping, and fine buildings. Although the estate was purchased in 1924 by the Sisters of Mercy for a college campus, it has retained its amazing ambience with few major changes, and as such is a striking example of how the very rich lived at the turn of the century.

Jay Gould, as most American history books tell us, was one of the most successful and ruthless of the great industrialists of the post–Civil War era, when mining and railroad monopolies dominated the business landscape. Gould's remorseless wheeling and dealing created a $1.5 million empire, reportedly making him the richest man in America. When he died in 1892, he left a large amount of his money to his son, George Jay Gould, as well as vast holdings in railroads and Western Union.

George, as the new head of the family, undertook to continue his father's daring business practices and excessive way of life. In competition with E. H. Harriman, another railroad magnate, he bought railroads throughout the country, expanding his holdings and challenging other railroad monopolies, such as the Pennsylvanian Railroad. By the turn of the century he seemed to have a transcontinental rail system within his grasp.

During this heady period he discovered Lakewood, New Jersey, where other industrialists' families like the Rockefellers already had homes, and he decided to build the equivalent of an eighteenth-century Georgian palace there. Despite finding himself amid many shaky financial deals and floating debts that were eating into the profits of his empire, he decided to forgo his father's Wall Street existence and become a "country gentleman" with a string of polo ponies and a new lifestyle. To accomplish this transformation, he had the thirty-room Georgian Court built for himself and his large family.

Georgian Court took shape on 200 acres of land at the edge of Lake Carasaljo in Lakewood. Bruce Price, a well-known architect, designed the gray mansion with a great conservatory, as well as stables for the many horses and twenty-one carriages of various types. A "Casino" was added; it was both an amphitheater and guesthouse with twenty extra bedrooms. Surrounding these structures was an exceptionally elegant landscape for sporting (some of the first private tennis courts in the nation were built here), indoor and outdoor polo grounds, three bowling alleys, a huge indoor swimming pool, a golf course, a gymnasium, and a Turkish bath. All of this was completed by 1899, when Gould brought guests to see it on a private train from New York. The estate was landscaped with an unusually fine collection of Italianate and Classical-style plantings, sunken flowerbeds, a Japanese teahouse (added in 1925), allées, neoclassical statuary, fountains, wide marble steps, and other elegant additions that added to the palatial aura of Georgian Court. Among the eye-catching wonders of this landscape is a giant fountain statue of Apollo by John Massey Rhind.

But Gould's empire was based upon unsound financing. His entire railroad system crashed in the Panic of 1907, and by nine years later all of his railroads had been lost. In 1924 his son, Kingdon Gould, put Georgian Court up for sale. It became the elegant college campus we see today, with only a few changes: among them the indoor polo field became an assembly hall, the Roman nudes were clothed, and one part of the stables burned down while the rest became a dining hall and classrooms. Thus the palatial playground of the nineteenth-century industrial baron met the twentieth century in a new guise.

A walk through this campus is a great pleasure both visually and historically, for it is hard to think of another site in our state that so captures the grandeur and folly of the robber-baron era. But here the scene is laid out so gracefully that it almost seems like a public park; it is hard to conceive of an owner designing such a site just for his own family's pleasure.

27·
TWIN LIGHTS
OF NAVESINK

Twin Lights of Navesink

*Exploring a Historic Lighthouse
and Center of Invention*

❧ HOW TO GET THERE

Take the Garden State Parkway to exit 117. Take Route 36 toward Highlands. Turn right just before Highlands Bridge to Sandy Hook, and look for Portland Road. Bear right onto Highlands Avenue and follow signs to Twin Lights.

❧ INFORMATION

Twin Lights lighthouse, museum, and tower are open daily from 10 A.M. to 5 P.M., from Memorial Day through Labor Day; and Wednesday through Sunday, 10 A.M. to 5 P.M., from September through May. The grounds are open until sunset. We recommend visiting on a clear day. Closed on New Year's Day, Thanksgiving, and Christmas. Guided tours are available. Telephone: 732-872-1814; Web site: www.twin-lights.org.

❧ Twin Lights is a historic site as both a lighthouse and lifesaving station and as an unusual place of science and invention. A visit here will fascinate children and adults alike. The walking aspect of your visit may be more vertical than our usual outings—you can climb to the top of the north tower of this interesting-looking building—but there is also a lovely flat stroll around its perimeter, with spectacular views of the water far below.

Twin Lights is situated on a bluff some 250 feet above the Shrewsbury River and Sandy Hook Bay. It is one of the highest spots on the eastern seaboard. When Henry Hudson came upon this spot in 1609 he described it as "a very good land to fall with, and a pleasant land to see." In fact, the use of this land for a beacon dates back to 1746, when the first warning system was set up here to protect Monmouth County and New York City from possible invasion. If five or more hostile-seeming vessels approached the coast, the beacon was illuminated, and an observer across the bay in New York was alerted.

But it was not until 1828 that the first lighthouse was erected. A year later a semaphore tower was erected, too, for the purpose of relaying messages from ships at sea to the Merchant's Exchange in New York.

It was in 1841, however, that this lighthouse made history; under the direction of Commodore Perry, a Fresnel lens was installed. This French invention was much stronger than previous beacon illuminations, and when both a stationary and revolving lens were added, Twin Lights became the most powerful lighthouse on the eastern seaboard, and was of particular importance to New York Harbor. Its beacons were visible for 70 miles.

The U.S. Life Saving Service was founded in 1848 for the purpose of rescuing shipwreck victims from the New Jersey coast. Twin Lights at Navesink was one of its stations. Today, Twin Lights is the only remaining station of the eight Life-Saving Service boathouses. The Boathouse at Twin Lights, erected in 1849, is still here to visit.

Today's lighthouse, with its two odd towers, was built in 1862 on the site of the original beacon. Twin Lights was designed by Joseph Lederle, and made of local brownstone. Though they are called twin towers, the north tower is octagonal, and the south tower is square; each rises to 64 feet. The two side-by-side beacons gave a distinctive signal to ships at sea, identifying immediately their location. The towers were connected by eighteen rooms for the keeper's and crew's housing (today mostly filled by the museum).

By 1883 the first lamps to burn kerosene were installed at Twin Lights. And then in 1898 an enormous (nine feet in diameter) electric light replaced the beehive-type light in the south tower. The Lighthouse Service built a generator to illuminate it. Today you can visit the building at the south of the complex to see the extraordinary light that revolves there. (The light was so bright that the north tower light was discontinued in 1962.)

Another major invention concerned Twin Lights as well. In 1899 Guglielmo Marconi decided to demonstrate his invention of the wireless telegraph at the lighthouse. He placed an antenna and receiving station at the site and reported by telegraph on an America's Cup yacht race at sea. His demonstration proved successful, enabling the *New York Herald* to scoop the outcome before anyone else. After this successful demonstration, Marconi created the nation's first wireless telegraph station at Twin Lights. By the 1920s the United States Army was also using the Twin Lights site for experimental electronics, including radar.

By the World War II era, however, new technology had been developed, including automated lights. In 1949 Twin Lights was decommissioned. But in 1962 it became a historic site, and today it is well worth a visit.

Begin your walk at the museum and a climb up the north tower. The museum has a large collection of artifacts and documents, in addition to a replica of Marconi's telegraph equipment. The collection of photos and equipment of the U.S. Life Saving Service is one of the best anywhere. Don't miss the Francis Life Car, an iron "vessel" that was used to bring people ashore from shipwrecks. Climb the north tower, which, though decommissioned, still blinks from dawn to dusk. This is the vertical part of the walk; there are sixty-four narrow, steep steps. The view is, of course, magnificent. Walk around the perimeter of the complex and visit the amazing nine-foot light and the boathouse with its replica of the lifesaving boats of the past. This site offers a rare combination of electronic invention and maritime history and adventure, brought quite brilliantly to life by the setting and exhibits. The giant light is mesmerizing, particularly for those of us who think of lighthouses as small glowing dots on the horizon.

☙ IN THE VICINITY

At Sandy Hook, a wonderful ocean-front beach and hiking area, you'll find **Fort Hancock** and **Spermacetti Cove.** Fort Hancock, a U.S. Army Proving Ground between 1874 and 1919, and a coastal defense fort, is today a collection of matching buildings in an idyllic setting, housing various research programs. At Spermacetti Cove from July through September you can watch park rangers and volunteers dress up and reenact U.S. Life Saving drills on the beach, with full shipwreck equipment. Telephone: 732-872-5970.

28·
ALLAIRE

Allaire Village

*A Deserted
Nineteenth-Century Village
and Company Town*

❧ HOW TO GET THERE

Take the New Jersey Turnpike to the Garden State Parkway and get off at exit 11. Take Route 195 west. Go to the second exit on 195, which is exit 31B. Allaire State Park, where the village is located is off Route 524 east, with the entrance on your right.

❧ INFORMATION

The village is open from 10 A.M. to 5 P.M., Monday to Saturday, and noon to 5 P.M. on Sunday, year-round except during January and February. The village is part of the larger (3,000 acre) state park, which has hiking and nature walks, golf, cross-country ski trails, and camping facilities. Telephone: 732-938-2253; Web site: www.allairevillage.org.

❧ Allaire, which was originally built around a bustling iron forge called the Williamsburg Forge, has a long history beginning around 1763. By 1814 this picturesque spot in Monmouth County had become a vibrant and very busy bog iron center, producing iron cauldrons, pots, pipes, stoves, and other objects.

By 1822, one Benjamin Howell joined forces with a brass founder named James Allaire to establish the Howell Works on the site. They employed some four hundred people in bog iron production. (Bog iron was produced by decaying vegetation.) By 1837 the community contained about sixty buildings. The village was a thriving success until the opening of the West introduced higher-grade iron ore and improved smelting systems. By mid-century Allaire's forge was closed down, and shortly thereafter the village was abandoned.

Through the generosity of the twentieth-century owner, Mrs. Arthur Brisbane, and the help of the Boy Scouts and other local organizations, the empty village and its surrounding woodlands and marshes were saved for today's walkers and history buffs. Only a few of these industrial communities of the past are still extant in New Jersey.

Strolling among the well-tended buildings and green lawns of the empty village we feel as though we have jumped back in time to the mid-nineteenth century. But as we walk through the bucolic and picturesque village today, we have to imagine the incredible noise (the iron smelter roared day and night) and the overwhelming odor and heavy, acrid smoke caused by the charcoal pits that made the fuel for the furnace. Also in operation, and providing both noise and pollution, were a sawmill, a gristmill, a blacksmith shop, and a screw factory, which employed the children of the village. Many of the workers toiling at these hard and grimy jobs were paid only in scrip, which they then spent in the several company stores of the village.

Though it is difficult to imagine these hard conditions, our visit to Allaire creates an unusually accurate sense of a nineteenth-century company town. There is also a narrow-gauge steam train, the Pine Creek Railroad, running at Allaire; its desolate whistle adds to the ambience of the past.

You will find the buildings at Allaire surprisingly far apart. Only about twenty of the original sixty structures still exist. Their restoration is not in the least "hokey"; each building has been carefully refurbished. Most are closed, though the General Store is open for visitors when the village itself is open. If you call for information you will find that many events demonstrating crafts and material culture of the past, such as cider making, candle dipping, and quilting, are scheduled. The steam train takes riders on a brief trip as well.

Begin your walk at the entrance to Allaire. As you wander on this slightly hilly pathway, where there are no vehicles and few people, note the surrounding woodland. And hike in it if you wish. No doubt the villagers hunted for rabbits here, and chopped wood for their fires. It is somewhat marshy—this is part of the Manasquam Floodplain Trail—so wear stout shoes.

On your walk you will come to the homes built by Mr. Allaire for his workers in about 1832. There is a building with exhibits and information. Pick up a self-guiding map here, or take an official tour if you prefer.

The next building is the foreman's cottage, dating to 1827. Note the simple and charming village architecture. Nearby is the entrance to the adjacent woodlands, with a nature trail, a bridge over a brook, and the site of the original sawmill. In the grinding mill and screw factory, the iron items produced in the village were ground and polished. Note the gristmill and blacksmith shop, which date to the 1930s. Continue on your walk and you'll find the old bakery; the upstairs of this building housed the village schoolroom. James Allaire paid for the school out of his own pocket, we are told. One of the oldest buildings is the manager's house, which was constructed as early as 1798 for the stagecoach driver.

The one business that is functioning whenever the village is open to visitors is the General Store. Filled with all kinds of items and goodies, this emporium reminds us of the importance of the old-fashioned community store. The carpentry shop and enameling building are next along the path. You'll find exhibits of the various crafts practiced in Allaire's heyday in the enameling building.

Soon you'll come to the furnace stack, the most historically important of the sites at Allaire, for this is the last remaining iron furnace in the state. The furnace was powered by a waterwheel, but today only the stack remains. The dormitory for the iron workers (one of the original buildings at the site) is nearby. Mr. Allaire himself lived there with his workers—certainly an unlikely situation for a factory owner today. The carriage house, hay barn, and cattle barns are next as you continue on the path through the village.

And finally, you will come to the charming Christ Church, an Episcopalian church built in the 1830s.

There are foundations and remains of other buildings at Allaire, and the interested walker can delve more deeply into the history of this quintessentially American small town by visiting the library and exhibits.

❧ IN THE VICINITY

Allaire is near the Atlantic coastline. There are several interesting and historic sites nearby.

At **Spring Lake** (take Route 524), you'll find one of the prettiest seaside towns on the Jersey shore. There are several historic sites of interest, including the **Osborn Farmhouse** (1840) at 412 Sussex Avenue; the octagonal **Portuguese Pavilion** (at 207 Atlantic Avenue); the **Missouri State Building** (at 411 Ocean Road); the massive hotels along the waterfront; and the **Atlas Home** (at 410 Passaic Avenue). There is an inexpensive visitor's trolley that, in one-half hour, takes you to see these sites and many others; it leaves Monday through Friday from Third and Morris avenues on the hour and half hour from 10 A.M. to 3:30 P.M.

Also along the coast is the village of **Ocean Grove**, which is well worth a visit. This historic town was founded by Methodists in the nineteenth century. See walk 29 for more about it.

29·
OCEAN GROVE

Ocean Grove Great Auditorium

A Victorian Camp Meeting Village on the Shore

❦ HOW TO GET THERE

Take the New Jersey Turnpike to exit 11 onto the Garden State Parkway, exit 100B. Take Route 33 east. Follow signs to Ocean Grove.

❦ INFORMATION

Ocean Grove is a bustling summer resort, as well as a continuing Methodist Camp destination in August. We recommend visiting in the off-season, if you want to stroll quietly through the village (and along the beach), but there is a lot going on year-round here, including many historic festivals and events. You can pick up a map of the village at any realtors and at many of the shops on Main Avenue, as well as at the Chamber of Commerce at 45 Pilgrim Pathway (near the Great Auditorium). Telephone: 800-388-4768; for a walking tour, 732-774-1869; Web site: www.oceangrovenj.com.

❦ The village of Ocean Grove is a one-of-a-kind shore community. It is a picturesque town with rows of small, well-kept Victorian homes, and a vast central architectural wonder—the Great Auditorium. Rows of elegant tents, occupied in season by Methodists, still border the auditorium. Some say there are more authentic Victorian homes in this town than in any other village in the United States. A fine, wide promenade runs the length of the village along the Atlantic coast. You will not find a similar enclave anywhere else on the Jersey shore. The village is both a scenic delight, and a historically well-kept and fascinating reminder of the many religious groups that created lasting communities in the state.

After the Civil War, residents of the growing urban centers of the East were seeking get-away places in the summer. In many cases they were drawn to the idea of a community that had shared beliefs, and that was both "physically and spiritually healthful." A group of Methodists from Philadelphia was looking for just such a site. Ocean Grove's lovely setting on the ocean—with its high beach, thick groves of pines and hickory, its absence of mosquitoes, and its isolation—appealed to its founders, a group of thirteen Methodist ministers under the direction of Dr. William B. Osborne, and thirteen laymen.

In 1869, they came in their carriages from Philadelphia to conduct a revival meeting. Methodist camp meetings were usually open-air revivals that drew large crowds and lasted for many days. At Ocean Grove they pitched their tents in this quiet spot, eventually creating a seaside resort in which to pursue annual summer camp meetings in relative isolation. Bounded on three sides by water (there are small lakes both north and south of the village), Ocean Grove provided them with a site that was "removed from the dissipations and follies of fashionable water places." They elected one Elwood H. Stokes as president of the Ocean Grove Camp Meeting Association. (You will see a statue of him in the village.) By 1874 the tent community, known as "little canvas village," included some two hundred ministers at the height of the season, and about seven hundred tents. These semi-permanent buildings, which have now lasted more than a century, had their own floors and small kitchens. There are still 114 of them, many having been passed from generation to generation. But many of the nineteenth-century Methodists opted for more permanent homes in the village; soon members were building the hundreds of small, quaint Victorian-style cottages that make this community a historic architectural treasure.

The Methodist Camp Association, which ran the community, remained a private organization so that it could maintain strict control over its members. Lots were leased for ninety-nine years. Strict rules included no alcohol, smoking, organ grinders, peddlers, vendors, carriages on the beach; no swearing in the boats on adjacent Lake Wesley; and, on Sundays, no wheeled vehicles, newspapers, dancing, or card playing. The gates (through which you will still enter the village) were closed promptly at 10 P.M., and remained tightly shut on Sundays. Visitors on Sundays had to enter over a footbridge from next-door Asbury Park. Trains were not allowed to stop at Ocean Grove on Sundays, either. President Ulysses S. Grant, who once visited his mother and sister on a Sunday at their rented Ocean Grove cottage, was obliged to walk into town, like any other pilgrim.

The few recreational activities allowed at Ocean Grove included boating on the sea and lakes, and promenading by the shore; the town fathers considered banning swimming because of the immodest disrobing it entailed, but they reluctantly agreed to allow it, except on Sundays.

However, the major activities at Ocean Grove did not involve the seaside and the charming setting. The Great Auditorium, an immense and curious structure—almost the size of a football field—was built in 1894 to accommodate 10,000 people and a choir of five hundred. It was here that the residents of the community congregated. The auditorium is unusual both in its architectural design, and for the fact that it was constructed without nails, in imitation of Solomon's temple. Here, during camp meetings, religious services were conducted daily, on a continuous basis. Ocean Grove still holds numerous religious and musical events in the Great Auditorium. Although some of its blue laws have disappeared over time—in 1980 courts ruled that such prohibitions constituted a conflict between church and state—the village retains a quaint, pristine quality that is hard to find elsewhere. Woody Allen set his movie *Stardust Memories* here.

As you walk through the village you'll find it is a fine example of nineteenth-century planning. The Great Auditorium is quite central, with a large grassy space around it. The rows of tents and streets of small houses are carefully laid out, with the buildings nearest the sea constructed the farthest back from the street. This arrangement created a funnel-like way for ocean breezes to reach the rest of the village, and allowed residents to sit on their porches and enjoy both views and sea air.

Of particular historic interest, of course, is the Great Auditorium, a giant edifice. It has a famous organ that is played twice weekly, and many interesting sights are within. Among the numerous illustrious visitors to the building have been seven presidents (Grant, Garfield, Theodore Roosevelt, Taft, Wilson, and Nixon), many governors, opera singers, and public figures. You can find a list of them at the Chamber of Commerce, where you can pick up a map of the village.

You will want to walk all around the Great Auditorium to see both the building itself and the rows of tents that surround it. Other nearby sights to see include Thornley Chapel (1889), the Bishop James Tabernacle (1877), the Beersheba Well (1870), and the Centennial Cottage (1874). In addition to these religious sites, be sure to see the many quaint streets of Victorian homes, including Pilgrim Pathway, Central Avenue, and the streets parallel to Ocean Avenue, which is the main thoroughfare along the shore. Don't miss Ocean Pathway, too—a picture-postcard Victorian street lined with trees and park benches. Main Avenue is a bustling street of small shops and restaurants. To re-create the Sunday isolation of Ocean Grove with its original blue laws, walk across the small footbridge over Wesley Lake.

30·
CATTUS ISLAND
AND
BARNEGAT LIGHT

Cattus Island

The Shore's Heritage
of Pirates and Patriots

𝔜 HOW TO GET THERE

Cattus Island

From Toms River, take Route 37; go north on Fischer Boulevard to Cattus Island Road on your right.

Barnegat Light

Take the Garden State Parkway to exit 67; at light go left onto West Bay Avenue and over the parkway to Route 9. Turn right (south) on Route 9 to the bridge to the island at Route 72 and north on Route 607 to the lighthouse.

𝔜 INFORMATION

Cattus Island is a county park and has an excellent interpretive center. Telephone: 732-270-6960; Web site: www.co.iceab.nj.us/parks/default/htm. Barnegat lighthouse can be visited. Telephone: 609-494-2016; Web site: www.njlighthousesociety/http/njhls/burlco.org.

𝔜 The story of New Jersey's pirates is one of both historic patriotism and swashbuckling adventure. The low-lying tidal marshes and hidden inlets of this coastal region were prime settings for stealth and attack, while the rushing currents of the Atlantic shoreline brought regular disaster to ships at sea. From the earliest period of American shipping, pirates and privateers preyed on the Jersey coast, while occasionally doing their patriotic best for the Revolutionary cause.

A few sites are of particular interest today, though it is hard to imagine our tourist-clogged coastline harboring dangerous pirates with lanterns, creeping through the marshes at night to attack sailing ships plying the waters along the coast. But this was always dangerous sailing, with shoals and strong currents; until recently there were wrecked ships not far from shore that could still be seen.

We have chosen two spots that were once noted for their danger and their piracy.

Cattus Island is just north of Toms River. This is an excellent spot to walk on a pleasant boardwalk that winds through the tidal marsh out toward Barnegat Bay. (It is called an island because it is cut off from the mainland in very high tides.) Here, amid the mysterious, often eight-foot-high reeds known as phragmites, is a setting that was well known to pirates during the Revolutionary War. You can easily imagine the salt marshes being used by privateers and patriots during that war, as they lay in wait in these hidden inlets and then attacked British ships, and unloaded their cargoes in the dead of night. These marshes are still empty and bleak, particularly as dusk falls, and it is easy to imagine small boats in these strange, brackish, marshy waters, completely hidden by the waving reeds. If you are also a nature lover, by the way, this is a great spot to see seabirds and some three hundred different types of vegetation, in addition to the phragmites. Walk out on the boardwalk to its farthest reach into the marshes for the best sense of this most unusual and historic landscape.

Not too far down the coastline is **Barnegat Light,** a favorite destination for lighthouse enthusiasts and beachgoers. Long Beach Island, of which Barnegat is the northern point, was made more accessible to tourists once a bridge to the mainland was constructed in the 1800s. But before that the island was known as home to the Barnegat Pirates or "wreckers" or "mooncussers," who preyed on the busy shipping area on moonless nights. Ships to and from New York sailed close to the shore to cut their time, and thus were easy prey for the pirates who lurked on the island.

The pirates themselves fell into several brackets. Some received a "letter of marque" from the Continental Congress, granting them license to become "legal" pirates who were free to capture British ships. Others simply kept and sold the goods of any ship they captured; privateering was a well-known route to money making. Some were Tory sympathizers who raided nearby farms and businesses in the nearby Pine Barrens (pine robbers), or robbed American ships that had run aground in bad weather.

Many of these adventurers worked off Long Beach Island, waiting for moonless nights and tricking unsuspecting captains by waving lanterns back and forth to simulate a settlement, or another ship that might have found a better route. By the time the ship had run aground on shoals, and perhaps broken into pieces, the pirates were already on their way to loot its cargo. (Similar tales abound off Cape Cod and Cape Hatteras, by the way.)

In 1835 the first lighthouse was constructed at Barnegat. It was 40 feet tall and marked the very hazardous coast line that had caused so many ships to founder. The lighthouse has a long history since then, including being used as a lookout in World War I. It was taken over by the Coast Guard in World War II and elegantly restored in 1988. You can climb the

217 winding steps of the lighthouse if you wish, and look out on the 18 miles of Long Beach Island. Or you can walk along the beach here and contemplate the history of piracy for which the Jersey Shore became so well known.

IN THE VICINITY

The **Sea Captains' Cemetery** in Barnegat and the **Barnegat Lighthouse History Museum** are both relevant sites. At the museum, a former one-room schoolhouse, you'll find the original lens of "Old Barney," as well as relics, photos, and documents of Barnegat's history.

31·
DOUBLE
TROUBLE AND
WHITESBOG
VILLAGES

Cranberries being picked by hand. From Harper's Weekly, *1877*

Cranberry Towns
in the Pinelands

❦ HOW TO GET THERE

Double Trouble State Park

From the Garden State Parkway take exit 80. Turn left (south) onto Double Trouble Road and go about 3 miles to entrance at end. Cranberry Village is just beyond the entrance.

Whitesbog Village

The village is in Lebanon State Forest. Take exit 67 off the Garden State Parkway to Route 554 west. Drive to Route 72, and take it to intersection with Route 70. Take 70 east to Route 530 and go left. Follow signs to entrance on your right.

❦ INFORMATION

Double Trouble Village is open daily. We suggest you pick up a self-guiding map of the village at the entrance. Telephone: 908-341-6662 or 908-793-0506; Web site: www. state.nj.us. dep/forestry/parks. Whitesbog village is also open daily. Pick up a self-guiding map at the Company Store in the village. Telephone: 609-893-4646; Web site: www. whitesbog.org.

❦ Cranberries were (and still are) a big business in New Jersey. The state's cranberry farms were centered around cranberry villages, designed to sort, process, and dry harvested cranberries for market. Each village had a major building, sometimes known as screenhouses, where good berries were screened from bad. There were also living quarters for workers, a general store, a foreman's house, a schoolhouse, and other typically nineteenth-century village needs. Two of these cranberry villages have been preserved—both within state parks in the Pinelands. A visit to one or both provides a glimpse of one of the rural enterprises that dotted the Pinelands in the nineteenth and early twentieth centuries.

Double Trouble (apparently named for the problems caused by muskrats making holes in the dams of the region) is a 5,000-acre state park encompassing two major bogs where the cranberries grew, and a dry, higher area between them, where the village is set. The first major industry on the site was a sawmill (there is still a sawmill to be seen here), and by 1866 its proprietor, the William Gilberson family, employed some 2,500 people in this remote spot. They produced shingles and timbers for ships among other wooden items. As the swamps emptied of trees, however, a new enterprise was needed, and they were planted with cranberry plants.

By 1909 it had become the Double Trouble Cranberry Company owned by the Edward Crabbe family; timber was processed in the off-season, and cranberries (and some blueberries) in the growing season. It was soon one of the largest cranberry operations in the state, and it continued to provide fresh cranberries to the market into the 1960s.

But the system for harvesting of the berries changed, making Double Trouble (and other such cranberry locations) obsolete. No longer was the big sorting and screening house with its hand-sorters needed, as new separating processes were employed. In 1964 the state purchased the operation, and still leases some of the area to cranberry farmers (you can see them at work in the nearby cranberry bogs in season). The state remains a major cranberry producer, but villages like this one and Whitesbog are now historic mementos of a past agricultural way of life.

Today Double Trouble Village has twelve structures in a self-contained village. A walk through the main street (buildings are not open to the public) will be a trip through time: the 1890 schoolhouse is the oldest building, the general store and bunkhouse date to 1900, and the sawmill (originally powered by a steam engine using creek waters) was constructed between 1906 and 1909. The great cranberry screenhouse was built between 1909 and 1916. You'll also see a bunkhouse and cookhouse, packers' cottages, and a foreman's house. As the map will tell you, each building had a specific purpose, and many were still in use in 1974.

Whitesbog is the other cranberry village that we recommend. Here, too, you can enjoy the ambience of a small Pine Barrens agricultural industry and the community that was created around it. The village is listed as both a National and State Historic Site. Whitesbog is being partially restored and has a variety of events for the public. There is an Old Bog Nature Trail and the Whitesbog Village Tree Trail, where you can see the Pine Barrens' great varieties of trees.

The village was originally built by the J. J. White Company in the 1860s; by the early 1900s Whitesbog had become the largest cranberry farm in New Jersey. In addition to year-round workers, some six hundred Italian immigrants were hired seasonally, and appropriately were housed in two small villages called Florence and Rome. The eldest daughter of the family, Elizabeth White, began working on the farm in the 1890s, and, working with wild blueberries, went on to develop a strain of blueberries to be farmed. She became a major agricultural force in the cranberry industry. The village and the 3,000 acres surrounding it are a fascinating testament to agricultural life a century ago. With your self-guiding map in hand, you can visit the Company Store (open to the public), the packing facility, and the machine shop, among many other buildings. There is a nineteenth-century canal that was used to supply water to the bogs, as well as the various trails noted above. An active preservation society is restoring buildings, while major cranberry and blueberry companies continue to farm the land around the village.

32·
LAKEHURST

Lakehurst Naval Air Station

The Naval Air Station,
the History of Flight,
and the Hindenburg Disaster

🎸 HOW TO GET THERE

Take exit 7 on the New Jersey Turnpike to Route 195 east. Take Route 571 south at exit 16. You'll see the Naval Air Station just before you reach Lakehurst.

🎸 INFORMATION

The only way to visit this most interesting site is by appointment, which should be done at least two weeks beforehand. For security reasons, it is impossible to enter the station without preregistration, and you must take a tour. Telephone to register: 732-818-7520; Web site: www.nlhs.com. Tours are given on the second and fourth Saturdays of each month, and Wednesdays from 10 A.M. to 2 P.M., except for holidays. Tours begin at 10 A.M., and include the New Navy Lakehurst Information Center, Historic Hangar One, the Air Park, and the Hindenburg Crash Site Memorial Marker.

🎸 Anyone with an interest in the history of flight will find this a remarkable visit. From the moment you spot the two giant—and this word is not to be taken lightly—buildings in the distance, you realize you are in for a most unusual experience. The station is vast, very military in ambience, and filled with everything to do with the history of planes and blimps and air travel. In historic Hangar #1 (built in 1921) you'll see all sorts of models, artifacts, and memorabilia from the LTA (Lighter-than-Air) era. While the base is particularly famous for the crash of the *Hindenburg* (see below), there is much more to see as well. Read the history first, and then prepare to absorb a dizzying array of historic information and atmosphere.

In the 1920s the growth of commercial aviation spurred the development of all kinds of new aircraft. Ranging from rocket-propelled gliders to helicopters, from high-altitude balloon flights to dirigibles, new experiments in the world of air travel were constantly being pioneered. The Naval Air Station at Lakehurst was the site for a great deal of this experimentation, and still is.

Zeppelins, or blimps, as the public called them, were among the new inventions. Germany was in the forefront of air experimentation. In the 1930s the hydrogen-inflated *Hindenburg,* with four Daimler-Benz diesel engines propelling it, was among the newest and most sought-after zeppelins; it flew from Germany to South America and the United States. While a private company had developed the Zeppelin, it soon was taken over by the Nazi government. In 1936 it made ten round-trip flights to the United States from Germany, cruising at 78–80 miles an hour. The trip took fifty-two hours from Germany, and sixty-five going back. The cost was $720 per person, and the voyage was considered luxurious, smooth, and very quiet. Among the amenities were elegant dinners served on porcelain china, and music played on an aluminum piano.

A year later, the demand for seats was so high that the *Hindenburg* scheduled eighteen flights to America. Despite several dramatic crashes in the American lighter-than-air program (including the *Shenandoah,* which flew from Lakehurst across the country numerous times before its crash in 1925), Zeppelin travel was considered very safe. But there were known problems: the American government had refused to sell Nazi Germany helium for fear it would be used in the war effort. The Germans, therefore, powered the zeppelins with highly flammable hydrogen gas instead. Nonetheless, the *Hindenburg* made six crossings safely.

The *Hindenburg* flew to Lakehurst for the first time in 1936, when 100,000 people turned out to see its arrival in front of Hangar #1. There were thirty-six passengers and a crew of sixty-one. As the onlookers awaited its approach on a stormy day, the captain was advised not to land until the wind subsided, so the huge dirigible floated back and forth between nearby Toms River and New York City. Preparing at last to land in the evening, the craft hovered over Lakehurst, its cables were dropped, and then, suddenly, it burst into flame. The huge airship was consumed by fire within minutes. Passengers jumped from the burning craft, volunteer fire-fighters on the ground tried to rescue them, and hundreds of onlookers watched in horror. Sixty-two of the ninety-seven people aboard survived.

But the crash of the *Hindenburg* doomed future transatlantic flights on such wingless airships. This disaster was one of the milestones in aviation history, turning the minds of experimenters away from such inventions and toward other types of aircraft. Don't miss looking at the great variety of airships at this site.

✿ IN THE VICINITY

Not far away is the **Cathedral of the Air.** This fieldstone Gothic Revival chapel is near Hangar #1, and was built in 1931 as a memorial. There are many historic things to see at the chapel, including stained glass windows depicting George Washington, and a series of medallions commemorating the history of flight.

❧ OF SIMILAR INTEREST

Naval Air Station Wildwood Aviation Museum at Cape May Airport. This museum is dedicated to World War II airmen and displays vintage aircraft. Telephone: 609-886-8787.

Millville Army Air Field Museum, in Millville. Dedicated to the airfield's history as "America's first defense airport," this is where 1,500 pilots and 10,000 service personnel trained for World War II. Telephone: 856-327-2347.

Air Victory Museum, in Medford, 68 Stacy Haines Road. This huge setting for a collection of military and historic aircraft includes replicas of the Wright Brothers' craft and the *Spirit of St. Louis.* Telephone: 609-267-4488.

Aviation Hall of Fame and Museum of New Jersey, at Teterboro Airport. Aircraft, artifacts, and photos are displayed here—all testament to New Jersey's more than two hundred years of aeronautic history. Telephone: 201-288-6345.

Prospertown Schoolhouse, in Jackson at 95 W. Veteran's Highway. This one-room, 1890s schoolhouse includes blimp and dirigible memorabilia as well as cranberry sorters and other relics of the past. Telephone: 732-928-1200.

33·
HISTORIC
WALNFORD

Historic Walnford

A Mill Village Reflecting
250 Years of History

❧ HOW TO GET THERE

Historic Walnford is part of Crosswicks Creek Park in Upper Freehold Township. From the New Jersey Turnpike, take Route 195 east to Route 539 south. Take Holmes Mill Road (Route 27) to Walnford Road and follow signs.

❧ INFORMATION

Historic Walnford is open daily from 8 A.M. to 4:30 P.M. There are many special programs. An excellent self-guided walking tour map is available at the entrance. Historic Walnford is listed on the National Register of Historic Places. Telephone: 609-259-6275 or; Web site: www.monmouthcountyparks.com/parks/walnford.asp.

❧ For a very pleasant and informative walk with a truly historic feeling, visit this out-of-the-way restoration. Unlike most "restored" villages, Historic Walnford does not represent only a particular period. Instead, the decision was made to interpret the site over its long 250-year history, from its beginnings as a colonial farm village to its development as an important gristmill location in the nineteenth century. Located on the banks of Crosswicks Creek, Walnford was a natural spot for a water-driven mill, and much of its history reflects its busy industry. Your walk will bring you past the gristmill on the banks of the creek and a charming group of cottages, sheds, and barns, as well as many grassy expanses and lovely old trees. A number of buildings have been restored and are open, including the amazing mill itself, and Waln House, the mill owner's residence.

What is today Historic Walnford was in colonial times a plantation developed around the original gristmill. (It should be remembered that gristmilling was colonial America's first industry.) The village dates to 1734. The property was advertised for sale in 1772 in a newspaper ad. At that time its 180 acres contained not only the gristmill but also a sawmill, fulling mill, blacksmith shop, cooper's shop, the fine brick home and five tenant houses, and assorted farm buildings. There were two fruit orchards, one hundred plowed acres, and twenty-five acres of meadowland. In 1772, Richard Waln, an international merchant trader and owner of a commercial wharf in Philadelphia, purchased the entire village, beginning a family ownership that would last for two centuries.

Today historians speculate that Waln, who was a Quaker who sympathized with the British, hoped to have his family (he had a wife and six children) safely settled in rural Monmouth County before war broke out. He invested heavily in the village, repairing mills and building himself a large and imposing home. Walnford became his commercial base; he shipped flour, lumber, and farm commodities to Philadelphia, New York, and beyond. Boats carrying goods could navigate Crosswicks Creek to Philadelphia.

In 1799, Waln's son Nicholas and his wife Sarah took charge of the many enterprises at Walnford. The village's growth reflected the prosperity of the early federal period in America. Five nearby farms were acquired during Nicholas Waln's stewardship, and Walnford became a 1,300-acre site for increased production of grain, milling, and lumber. By 1848, fifty people lived in Walnford.

As the West opened up to larger farms and railroad transportation at midcentury, grain production and larger farms overtook the small New Jersey industry. At Walnford the various fields and industries were distributed to the wife and many heirs of Nicholas Waln when he died in 1848. While his widow and children made efforts to keep the town and farms profitable by mortgaging land and industry, economic changes in American life and a disastrous mill fire destroyed Walnford's prosperity. By the end of the nineteenth century, the sawmill, the blacksmith, and the cooper were gone, and the gristmill worked only for local businesses.

The village soon became the idyllic retreat for a Philadelphia family descended from the Walns. The mill pond, once the source of power for the mills, became a romantic setting for waterlilies and ornamental borders. While a dairy farm and the gristmill still operated, the setting became primarily a country estate.

The entire site was reduced to 48 acres by 1954. When it was sold in 1973 to Edward and Jeanne Mullen, the first owners who were not descendants of the Walns, they had it listed on the National Register, and subsequently donated the entire village to the Monmouth County Park System.

A walk through the village, using the self-guiding map, will take you from one interesting spot to the next in a short time. But there is a lot more to see than the exteriors of the buildings, for there are demonstrations of milling and exhibits of archaeological finds, as well as wonderful hikes throughout the wooded areas and meadowlands of Walnford.

You will begin your walk at the Corn Crib and the many farm buildings that suggest a working farm—from the production of grain and hogs to the stabling of standard-bred horses.

Nearby is the fully restored 1879 carriage house. It was added to the estate by the widow of Nicholas Waln.

The grove of white pines you come to next was planted in the early twentieth century, when viewing farm operations was no longer considered necessary. By this time Walnford had become more a country estate than a business proposition.

Waln House, the manorlike, Georgian-style home of the family, is next on your walk. Note the various changes that have been made over the centuries to the house, including the picket fence and front porch. Nearby, alongside the creek, is the formal garden.

The great gristmill is next, built in 1872 after fire destroyed the earlier building. Go inside for a careful and fascinating look at how a stone mill operated. You'll also see traces of the original mill, which stood on the opposite side of the creek.

Nearby are a few remains of the eighteenth-century tenant houses that once dotted the area next to the mill. Foundations of the smokehouse and blacksmith shop are in the same vicinity.

From here you will enter the meadows and farm lanes of Walnford, as well as the cow pasture and the cow barn, built in the early twentieth century and now housing a variety of programs and events. From this spot we recommend that you take advantage of the picturesque scenery to walk through the scenic area that surrounds the village.

Walnford's history can be seen as typical of the small family-owned American villages that dotted the area since the colonial era, adapting to the changing economic and cultural movements of the times. Fortunately, a few of them, like Walnford, were saved for us to experience.

34·
ROOSEVELT

*Portrait bust of Franklin Delano Roosevelt
by Jonathan Shahn, Roosevelt*

A New Deal Hideaway

❧ HOW TO GET THERE

Take exit 8 on the New Jersey Turnpike, to Route 33 west to Hightstown for a short distance. Pick up Route 571 south and take it to Roosevelt.

❧ INFORMATION

This is a very small village with hardly any public buildings and no town center. There is a post office, however, and you can get local directions there. But many tourists do visit the town, and the school where the artworks are located welcomes visitors. Visit during school hours, and ring the bell for admittance. The school is located on School Lane, just off Pine Drive. The Roosevelt Trail is just beyond the schoolyard.

❧ A visit to Roosevelt will remind those of us with memories of 1930s America of a time and place filled with both despair and idealism. For younger visitors, it is as close as they can come to seeing a genuine planned community that still functions and endures quite satisfactorily, much the way it has for some seventy years. The town of Roosevelt was a Depression-era experiment that brought about two hundred city-dwelling families to remote farmland in Monmouth County. The aim was to start a self-contained, idealistic community. What Roosevelt became is a story in itself—and today occasional busloads of tourists with cameras come from as far away as Japan to see how it worked, and still works. Now, more than half a century later, Roosevelt welcomes visitors as it attempts to live up to the high ideals of a long-ago time, in a contemporary world of commerce and urban sprawl.

The two square miles of Roosevelt were once farmland and forest, and today there is still a great deal of open, preserved space. The concept of the original town of Roosevelt seemed a simple one for aiding city-dwelling immigrants who were without work, and who could set up a cooperative village in unused space. Jersey Homesteads was one of the largest and first of the ninety-nine communities the federal government sponsored in a daring experiment into Depression-era social engineering.

Under the incisive guidance of Benjamin Brown, who was a leader of the Jewish agrarian movement (an idea that dated back to the nineteenth century), immigrants from the city would join him on his New Jersey farm and on additional acreage bought by the government, to set up an ideal community. Having convinced the government that his plan would work, Brown went through some 800 family applications and chose just 120. Almost all of them were Jewish garment workers from New York. Each of them contributed $500 to become settlers. A writer for the Works Progress Administration reported that "Jersey Homesteads is designed to find a simple and happy solution for the complexities of modern industrial life."

The first building constructed was a garment factory. The concept was not without detractors, among them David Dubinsky of the Ladies Garment Workers Union in New York. Albert Einstein, of nearby Princeton, was a major defender of the idea, and he talked to Dubinsky, who finally agreed when it was made clear that workers would turn out clothing only when it was needed, and revert to farming when it was not.

The town was laid out by a German-born exponent of the International Style, Alfred Kastner, and his assistant, Louis Kahn, who went on to become one of the twentieth century's most noted architects. The one-story, white stucco houses were constructed using Bauhaus principles of geometric simplicity. (Critics of the time said Jersey Homesteads looked like a village of garages.) Large areas of green space and forest land were incorporated into the community's design. Each family paid between $14 and $17 in rent per month for their corner of what seemed to them like Paradise after the crowded ghettos they had left behind in Europe. Between 1935 and 1938 about two hundred houses were built, soon supplemented by a cooperative store, community center, borough hall, school, and synagogue.

The entirely Jewish community was filled with ideologues, Zionists, anarchists, socialists, and artists, but few had farming or industrial experience. Both money-making enterprises failed after a few years. But the village continued to thrive. For those who lived there, the community was a philosophical home, a testament to shared values and commitments. In 1945 the village was renamed Roosevelt as a tribute to the president. It had become something of a left-wing artists' community after the arrival of Ben Shahn.

Shahn had been asked to paint a mural depicting the birth of the village. His 45-foot-long mural is a masterpiece of 1930s social-conscious art, depicting every element of the founding of the village, from Einstein's intercession to the laying of brickwork and the rows of sewing machines in the original factory. Shahn's brilliant evocation and his support for the village drew numerous other artists to Roosevelt. (The *New York Times* described Shahn as the nation's "official leftist artist.") "You get a lot of people who felt they didn't fit in anywhere and they came to Roosevelt and they felt welcome here," said the current mayor recently. And many second and third-generation family members stayed on.

With careful determination, today's Roosevelt citizens are trying to preserve that way of life despite the encroachments of the outside world. When you visit the community you feel you have walked back in time, even though the houses have been added to and decorated, and there is a small restaurant.

The school, where the Shahn mural is now proudly displayed, is a welcoming place, filled with art by notable residents. There is an impressive 1936 sculpture of a garment worker by Lenore Thomas. Don't miss a large and fascinating hammered aluminum wall relief by Otto Wester (1938) depicting garment workers and field workers alike. There are a series of woodcuts by Gregorio Prestopino, and prints by Jacob Landau. You'll find the atmosphere where today's Roosevelt students go to school both historic and artistic.

Walk behind the school to see the fine head of Franklin D. Roosevelt by Shahn's son, the sculptor Jonathan Shahn, who still lives in the community. And beyond the school ground is a forest walk, called Roosevelt Woodland Trail. We history lovers (and admirers of Bauhaus architecture) can only hope (and support) current efforts to keep Roosevelt such a special place.

35·
BORDENTOWN

Bordentown

Architectural Pleasures
from a Colonial Past
to the Bonapartes

❧ HOW TO GET THERE

Take exit 7 on the New Jersey Turnpike to Route 206. Follow signs to Bordentown; you will find the main street, Farnsworth Avenue.

❧ INFORMATION

For general information on historic sites, call the Downtown Bordentown Association at 609-298-3334. Bordentown offers Thomas Paine Walking Tours by calling 609-324-9909. Web site: www.downtownbordentown.com. For a local historian who can answer questions and guide your walk, stop in at the antique bookshop, "U and I," at 150 Farnsworth Avenue and speak with Arlene Bice. We suggest you leave your car on Farnsworth Avenue and do most of this outing on foot.

❧ Bordentown has a long history, beginning in colonial and Revolutionary times, when a number of important Americans—both political and artistic—lived there, and continuing into the nineteenth century when Napoleon's brother chose to make his home there. During much of that century, Bordentown, with its charming setting near the Delaware River, was a summer retreat for well-to-do visitors from Trenton and Philadelphia and even New York.

Architecture representing the entire history of Bordentown is easy to find here. Examples of Colonial and Federal architecture can be seen on Farnsworth Avenue, and fine homes, many in the French Empire style, still grace the bluffs just above the water. A walk through Bordentown will combine both history and an interest in architectural styles, though unfortunately many of the oldest buildings are now gone. Nevertheless, we recommend a stroll that will strongly suggest the various political and architectural eras in this charming town's history.

Bordentown was settled by a Quaker, Thomas Farnsworth, who had set up a trading post there by 1682. His original land included the northwest corner of Prince and Park Streets. Joseph Borden bought land from Farnsworth, and in 1717 designed the village; by 1740 he had opened both stagecoach and water routes connecting New York and Philadelphia through Bordentown.

A progressive thinker and enterprising colonist, Borden had notable friends who joined him in opposing the British yoke. Among the active colonists in Bordentown were Thomas Paine, the author of "Common Sense"; Francis Hopkinson, an artist and statesman and signer of the Declaration of Independence; and a submarine explorer named David Bushnell. It was Bushnell who had the idea of floating kegs of gunpowder down the Delaware River toward British ships in 1778. Though they did not explode, the episode thoroughly upset the British and occasioned the satiric poem by Francis Hopkinson that reads in part: "The cannon roar from shore to shore, / The small arms loud did rattle. / Since wars began, / I'm sure no man, / E'er saw so strange a battle." The Battle of the Kegs was just one of many skirmishes in Bordentown, a patriot stronghold, that was burned by the British several times. The house of Joseph Borden was among those destroyed.

After the Revolution, Bordentown's fine setting and air of calm and prosperity attracted Napoleon's exiled elder brother Joseph, the former king of Naples and Spain. The 1,800 acres he bought in the north end of town soon became the site of an elaborate palacelike estate, with extraordinary gardens and architectural wonders—now, alas, all gone. You can still see some of the garden structures in rock on your right, however, if you drive into the Divine Word Missionary complex on Park Street, but the area is private. Bonaparte had hired numerous artisans and artists to create designs and ironwork, thus setting somewhat of a Bordentown style that can still be seen in elaborate grillwork and gateways on the many nineteenth-century homes.

A number of engineers and inventions also played a part in Bordentown's history. Joseph Fitch's steamboat and the first steam locomotive in the nation were worked on at Bordentown; you'll spot a monument by the track in the center of town. The Delaware-Raritan Canal also bordered Bordentown; don't miss walking down the narrow road at the end of Farnsworth Avenue to see it today.

Bordentown has had a long and illustrious history as an art and literary colony, and as a center of education. You will see the home of Patience Lovell Wright and her son Joseph, both painters of note. Gilbert Stuart also lived for a time in Bordentown. The pastoral artist Susan Waters lived in town, as did the Gilder family; Richard Watson Gilder was the editor of the influential *Century Magazine.* Many schools were founded in the town, including the first tax-supported public school that has endured in New Jersey, which was started by Clara Barton, the founder of the Red Cross and a Bordentown resident. A school for black youth that became known as the Tuskegee of the North was started here, as was a military academy.

Our walking tour will touch on many of these elements of Bordentown's history, and with this overview in mind, you might begin your walk at the entrance to town at Crosswicks and Burlington Streets, where your first site is **Clara Barton's School** (moved to this location). It is open by appointment. Also on Crosswicks Street is the **Gilder House Museum**, also open by appointment. Part of the house dates to 1755, with an addition built in 1788.

Take Union Street to the main street, Farnsworth Avenue; you will pass a number of interesting architectural sites, including examples of Queen Anne–style houses, Victorian homes with Eastlake porches, and early twentieth century bungalow-style houses. At Farnsworth Avenue, your first building of note is at number 433, where you'll see the **Julian House**, which was one of the earliest private schools in town. The roof over the side door was taken from Washington's headquarters at Valley Forge, and there is a notable Greek Revival doorway. Number 428 is in the Italianate Villa style, with examples of the black iron grillwork that appears throughout town. Across from the 1869 Presbyterian Church is number 425, another example of late nineteenth century Italianate style. On the corner, **App's Hardware** will give you a taste of a shop of the past.

At 302 Farnsworth Avenue is the original **Old Friends Meeting House**, built in 1740. Joseph Borden had deeded the land to the Quakers for this simple building. Continuing along Farnsworth, you'll come to Church Street; one block to your left is Prince Street, and here you'll find an old and interesting cemetery, where some of the graves date back to the Revolutionary era. Also on Prince Street are 1820s and 1830s houses, and at 6 Prince Street is one of the major mansions of town, the 1840 Georgian-Federalist **McKnight House.**

Back on Farnsworth Avenue at the intersection of Crosswicks Street at number 11 Crosswicks is the **Old City Hall**, a notable building with its Queen Anne tower and original Seth Thomas clock, dedicated, by the way, to William F. Allen of Bordentown, who devised standard time. Also in the center of town, note the monument commemorating the first steam train that ran through Bordentown.

At the northwest corner of Farnsworth Avenue and Church Street is what at first glance is a somewhat nondescript building. Its upper story is original, and it is this house that Thomas Paine bought in 1777 just after he had written "Common Sense," his best-selling pamphlet that galvanized the colonists to revolution. Paine lived intermittently in Bordentown throughout the war, usually staying with friends and renting out his house. After war's end he began his scientific experiments, inventing such things as a smokeless candle and becoming interested in Fitch and Fulton's steam-boat engine. It was here that he devised his model of an iron railroad bridge, which would eventually be built in Britain. After a visit to France, where he was imprisoned by French Revolutionaries, in 1803 he came back to Bordentown but was denounced by religious groups for his "Age of Reason." Though he was booed and mistreated by a number of Bordentown citizens, he never gave up his belief in the right to free speech. The tavern and other spots that Paine frequented in Bordentown are now, unfortunately, gone.

However, several other buildings of the early era do remain, including the Hopkinson House at 63 Park Street at the corner of Farnsworth. This fine brick home was where the author of "Hail Columbia," Joseph Hopkinson, lived. By 1820 the house was owned by Bonaparte's doctor, and then it became part of the Bordentown Military Institute.

Across Farnsworth Avenue is the elegant **Francis Hopkinson House** at 101 Farnsworth. Built in 1750 by the patriot and signer of the Declaration of Independence, this house was altered over the centuries but is still a fine example of a grand eighteenth-century building. Note the original doorway and the date on the side of the house facing Park Street. The Bordens lived here after the Hessians destroyed their house.

At 100 Farnsworth Avenue, across the street, is the gracious Federal home of an early American artist, Patience Lovell Wright. A sculptor of some note, she was born to a Quaker family in Bordentown and lived in this house until 1769. Her son Joseph succeeded her as a successful artist. One of a number of artists who made this town their home (including Gilbert Stuart), Wright is considered the nation's first portrait sculptor. Her lifelike wax miniature portraits were much admired; among her subjects were George Washington and Benjamin Franklin. During a sojourn in England to make portraits of notable Britons, she moonlighted as a spy for the Americans. An example of her work can be seen at the Gilder House Museum. You'll find her grave at the cemetery on Prince Street.

A detour off Farnsworth Avenue to Second Street (to your right) and then to Mary Street will take you to the home of another Bordentown artist, Susan Waters. She lived in the black and white frame house set back into a garden; her pastoral works are in several museums.

At 32 Farnsworth Avenue is a beautiful Georgian house with extensive ironwork fences (note the wheat sheaves) and detailing, including iron columns. This is the **Joseph Borden House**, built on the site of his original home that was burned in 1775 as a retaliatory gesture by the British and Hessians. If you walk around this house you'll find a number of other interesting mansions in a variety of architectural styles, including Second Empire, Italianate, and Queen Anne. This town is a gem for those interested in architectural oddities of the past.

36·
BURLINGTON

Burlington

*New Jersey's Oldest
Colonial Streetscape
on the Delaware*

❀ HOW TO GET THERE

From the New Jersey Turnpike, take exit 5. Turn left onto Route 541 and go about three miles. Cross Route 130; you will enter Burlington on High Street.

❀ INFORMATION

The Library and the Historical Society both have self-guided walking tour maps. You'll find the Historical Society Headquarters at 12 Smith Lane, near the intersection of High Street and W. Broad Street. The Library Company of Burlington is at 23 West Union Street, just around the corner from the Historical Society. An audiotape describing historic sites is also available. Telephone: 609-386-0200 or 609-386-4773; guided tours are also offered: 609-386-3993; Web site: www.tourburlington.org.

❀ Burlington is the oldest European settlement in New Jersey. It has managed to preserve a large amount of its heritage—the oldest library, the oldest pharmacy, many of the oldest homes in the state and once the capital of New Jersey. It was one of the most important Quaker settlements in the region. A variety of events have placed it squarely in the center of many of the state's most historic happenings. Its Historic District encompasses forty sites of colonial interest (one square mile) in an unusually attractive setting for walkers. Burlington sits elegantly along the broad Delaware River, with a walkway along it, parks, and tree-lined, brick-cobbled streets filled with interesting sights. In clear view is Burlington Island, the site of the state's first settlement in 1624. We recommend this outing to any history buff or walker who wishes to get a true sense of what life in New Jersey's long-ago past was like. And even without the touristy addition of costumes and craftspersons dressed in eighteenth-century clothing, Burlington celebrates its past.

The first recorded settlement in the state was on Burlington Island, where, beginning in 1624, a trading post manned by Belgians bartered with local Indians. The earliest record of an African presence in the state is in a Dutch colonial reference to slaves in the mid-seventeenth century. The settlement passed through the hands of the Dutch, the Swedes, and the Finns, until the English took control in 1664. It became the first permanent settlement for Quakers fleeing persecution in Yorkshire and London; they laid out the town on the riverbank facing Burlington Island, originally calling it Bridlington or New Beverly. It became the leading Quaker settlement in the country, with William Penn visiting frequently from his own settlement just across the river. By the late seventeenth century, it was a flourishing colonial outpost, with its Friends Meeting House completed in 1683. (The present Meeting House dates to 1785, and is still in use; visit the burial ground behind it to see the graves of some of the earliest settlers.) In 1682 Burlington hosted the first meeting of the General Assembly of West Jersey, and five years later the Council of Proprietors met in the town.

It was in Burlington around 1726 that Benjamin Franklin used the first copperplate printing press to print New Jersey's original colonial currency. You can visit the Isaac Collins Print Shop where Franklin and other printers produced the earliest weekly newspaper in the state, almanacs, and Bibles, as well as currency. Burlington also has the first library still in continuous use in the state, the first firehouse in the state, the oldest pharmacy in continuous use in new Jersey, the oldest Episcopal Church, and one of the first African American churches in the state.

Burlington became a hotbed of patriot activity during the Revolution, and the home of several of the most important figures in the new American government, including Elias Boudinot, the first president of the Continental Congress, whose house can be visited. The grave of Oliver Cromwell, a black Revolutionary soldier, can be seen behind the Methodist Church.

During the nineteenth century, Burlington was home to a number of well-known personalities, including Captain James Lawrence, the War of 1812 hero who is famous for his "Don't give up the Ship!" exhortation; President Ulysses S. Grant, author James Fenimore Cooper, and several other notable figures. By the midcentury, as a Quaker and abolitionist stronghold, Burlington became a major stop on the Underground Railway; its location on the Delaware enabled fleeing slaves from southern states to cross the river into several welcoming homes in the village. (See walk 37.)

Numerous historic buildings remain, and many can be visited inside. There are also several interesting sites, such as notable churches and the Friends' Meetinghouse, graveyards, the Delaware River walkway, and even the island, where the first Burlington settlement was located. We suggest that you pick up a self-guiding tour map (see above), and note the general layout of the historic district; there are two major streets that intersect and several smaller ones to visit in even the shortest historic walking route. Using your map, be sure to visit High Street, West Broad Street, Union Street, and Riverbank, with its great view of the Delaware and the island.

On High Street, don't miss such colonial sites as **Hopkins House**, the **Isaac Collins Print Shop**, the **Pugh House** (once called the Counting House), the **Gardiner House, Alcazar** (dating to 1680), the **Smith House**, the **Blue Anchor Tavern** that has been serving guests since 1750, and the **Library Company of Burlington**. Also on High Street of later date but major interest are **Temple B'nai Israel** of 1801, the **Burlington Pharmacy** where runaway slaves were hidden, the **Friends' Meetinghouse** and grounds, and the **Endeavor Fire Company** with its antique spire. Additional sites of interest on High Street are the **Captain James Lawrence House** and the **James Fenimore Cooper House.**

On West Broad Street, important sites include the **Surveyor General's office** of 1676, the 1770 **Kinsey House**, the Federal style **McIlvaine House**, and the two **St. Mary's Episcopal churches** (one colonial and the other designed by the noted architect Richard Upjohn), the **St. Mary's Guild Hall**, and the **Biddle-Pugh House** and **Boudinot-Bradford House** of the early Federal period.

Union Street is the site of the **Oliver Cromwell House.** Cromwell was an African American Revolutionary War soldier who crossed the Delaware with General Washington. Also on Union Street is the 1839 **Costello-Lyceum Hall**, and between Union and York Streets you'll find the **Friends' Schoolhouse** dating to 1792.

Riverbank, with its lovely view, has several interesting locations to see. Of particular interest is the Victorian-style **Grubb Estate**, facing the river, which reportedly had a tunnel to the river that was used by the Underground Railway, and the Gothic Revival Shippen and Riverbank Houses. Near Riverbank, on Pearl Street is the **Bethlehem African Methodist Episcopal Church**, founded in 1855. Also on Pearl Street is the 1685 **Revell House**, reportedly the oldest house in this part of the state.

There are other sites of interest as well. The island where the first settlement in Burlington was located can be reached by boat from the ramp at York Street (off Riverbank). As you will see from the Historical Society map, you can drive to additional historic sites. But the walking tour, on brick sidewalks, is easily accomplished, and you can leave your car and enjoy the most fascinating of history walks in this town.

🌼 IN THE VICINITY

Don't miss a visit to nearby **Crosswicks.** Also a Quaker settlement, the tiny hamlet of Crosswicks has seen a lot of history, including a skirmish during the Revolutionary War and an important role in the Underground Railway. Called Crossweeksung by the Indians, it became the site of a mission in colonial times. In June 1778 the battle of a local militia with some Hessians soldiers took place at a small bridge in Crosswicks; you can still see bayonet marks and the eighteenth-century cannon ball that was lodged in the brick wall of the Quaker Meeting House in the center of a large and leafy town green.

37·
BURLINGTON
AND ITS
NEIGHBORS

The historic pharmacy in Burlington

Stops on the
Underground Railroad

❧ HOW TO GET THERE

Take the New Jersey Turnpike to exit 5; go left onto Route 541 for three miles. Cross Route 130; you will enter Burlington on High Street.

❧ INFORMATION

For information on African American history go to www.tourburlington.org: guide to African American sites. You can pick up a map of Burlington's Historic District at the library or Historical Society (see walk 36). Some of the following spots can be visited; check with the Historical Society. Telephone: 609-386-0200.

❧ Today the Underground Railroad—that series of secret hideouts that runaway slaves used to escape their bondage—is seen as an epic American story, pitting the forces of good and evil into moral combat. More and more homes and businesses and churches are being identified across the eastern half of the nation as having had a part in this extraordinary story. New Jersey, so close to the slave-owning states of Maryland, Virginia, and Delaware, was right in the middle of the routes that many escaping slaves took. Burlington County, with its position on the Delaware River, just across from Philadelphia, played a major role, with the town of Burlington a center of Abolitionist sentiment.

The Underground Railroad is now the subject of intense interest, though for more than a century it was hardly discussed. A carefully kept secret, its hidden stops were the subject of legends and folktales handed down from generation to generation. But it is now thought that an estimated 50,000 runaway slaves escaped through various routes north. New Jersey has a share of these havens, particularly in Quaker areas, for the Friends were staunch abolitionists and played a large role in the Underground Railroad in this state. Even the Quakers kept very quiet about their activities, using only word of mouth or written phrases such as "having overnight guests." Although New Jersey had outlawed slavery in 1846, it had, however, signed the Fugitive Slave Law in 1850, promising to return runaways to their owners. Thus runaways were often hesitant to stay in the state, though several all-black communities did exist. Most, however, continued north.

There was little Northerners could do about the vicious institution of slavery, but as runaway black men and women began arriving in the state in the 1840s and 1850s, many New Jerseyans—often at great risk to themselves—undertook to aid these fugitives to find a free and dignified life in the North. Both whites and free blacks already living in the state played a role. "Passengers" on the Underground Railroad were hidden, fed, clothed, and cared for at each "station" after their often harrowing escapes from the South. Even though the Quakers were the major force for abolition, others (many described as readers of Horace Greeley's *New York Tribune*) helped, too, often arranging for the Quakers to take charge of the runaways' passage from town to town.

There were several routes through the state. One route took the escaping slaves from Philadelphia, across the Delaware and into a series of Burlington County safe houses (see below) and on to Jersey City and New York. Another route crossed the Delaware in southern New Jersey around Salem, eventually connecting with the more northern route at Bordentown, and then on to New York. The third was known as the Greenwich Line, crossing the Delaware Bay near Greenwich, marked with yellow and blue lights, eventually arriving in Swedesboro and Mount Holly.

We have chosen to explore this route because a number of stops in Burlington County are identifiable and still within walking distance of one another. Following this brief walk is a series of stops in nearby towns, including Lawnside, Mount Holly, Mount Laurel, Moorestown, and Cherry Hill.

You can begin your walk at Riverbank Promenade on the Delaware River shoreline. From here, unless you are a boater, you will look out at Burlington Island, where a small community of Walloons from Belgium settled as early as 1624. New Jersey's first record of an African presence notes slaves of a Dutch official held here as early as 1659, who were subsequently resold as slaves to plantation owners in Maryland in 1664.

Parallel to Riverbank Promenade is Pearl Street. At 213 Pearl Street is Burlington's oldest African American institution, the **Bethlehem African Methodist Episcopal Church**, founded in 1830 and replaced with this building in 1855. Though not identified as a stop on the Underground Railroad, its very early existence indicates that many free blacks lived in the community, and were perhaps instrumental in the abolitionist cause.

From here take York Street into town and turn right at Union Street. On the corner of Union and Stacy streets at 114 E. Union Street you'll find the 1798 **Oliver Cromwell House,** where Cromwell, one of some five thousand black soldiers in the Revolutionary War, lived.

Continue on Stacy Street to East Broad Street, where you will turn right and walk to High Street. Turn right again. Your next stop is the **Friends Meeting House** at 341 High Street. This imposing building—in use for over three hundred years—was a center of local efforts to end slavery.

Just down the street at 302 High Street is the 1731 Burlington pharmacy, now called **Wheatley's Pharmacy.** The state's oldest pharmacy in continuous operation, it opened for business in 1842; it was owned by a strongly abolitionist Quaker named William J. Allinson. He used the site as a center for his antislavery rallies and invited famous abolitionists, including poet John Greenleaf Whittier, to speak from his doorstep. Tradition says that tunnels in the basement of the pharmacy provided shelter for runaway slaves.

Continue on High Street back toward the river, and at Pearl Street go left to Wood Street. The last house on your right is the **Grubb Estate** at 46 Riverbank. This house was owned by Henry Grubb, an ardent abolitionist; he is thought to have built the tunnels running from the riverbank to his basement for the rescue of runaway slaves. Grubb's estate had a number of buildings, including a tannery, a brewery, and a brickyard; it is not known what role they played in hiding the slaves at this stop on the Underground Railroad.

❧ For further Underground Railroad sites in nearby towns, visit the following:

Lawnside: Peter Mott House Museum, 26 Kings Court. One of the few Underground Railroad stops known today to have been operated by a free black man, the Peter Mott House is in Lawnside (then called Sugar Hill), the only all-black town on the Underground Railroad. Mott was a farmer and pastor, and perhaps a fugitive slave himself from Delaware. Telephone: 856-546-8850.

While in Lawnside, visit the **Mount Pisgah A.M.E. Church and Cemetery** on White Horse Pike.

Cherry Hill: Edgewater (at Croft Farm), Barton's Mill Road, off Brace Road. This lovely 1741 mansion was owned by a Quaker abolitionist, Josiah

Bispham; it became a safe house on the Underground Railroad. Fugitives from nearby Woodbury were hidden in the haymow and attic, and then sent on to Mount Holly. Telephone: 856-795-6225.

Mount Laurel: Evesham Friends Meeting House, Moorestown-Mount Laurel Road. This magnificent eighteenth-century stone building still functions as a Quaker meetinghouse, and is well worth a visit, both as a historical site and stop on the Underground Railroad and for its architectural beauty.

Also in Mount Laurel, **Jacobs Chapel A.M.E. Church**, 318 Elbo Land. Known to have played a role in the Underground Railroad, it dates to 1813, and is one of America's oldest black institutions. Telephone: 856-234-1728.

Moorestown: Elisha Barcklow House, 274 Main Street. This village house belonged to a Quaker and, according to oral tradition, was a station on the Underground Railroad. Moorestown is an unusually attractive and historic town. Visit the Historical Society in the Smith-Cadbury Mansion at 12 High Street to get a self-guided walking tour map.

38·
ROEBLING

Roebling

A Turn-of-the-Century,
One-of-a Kind Factory Town

❧ HOW TO GET THERE

From Route 295 take exit 57 (A or B) and Route 541, following signs to Roebling.

❧ INFORMATION

For information call the Roebling Historical Society at 609-499-7632; Web site: www.roeblinghistoricalsociety.org.

❧ America offers a number of planned communities one can visit. Some were created by Utopians or religious groups or by various far-thinking individuals who imagined a group living and working together harmoniously. But Roebling is a one-of-a-kind "company town" created by a noted family of industrialists and engineers. It was designed to be humanistic, self-contained, controllable, and profitable. It exists today much as it did in 1905, with housing in neat rows near communal spaces and amenities—but now without the central factory buildings behind its great industrial gates. A visit here is fascinating—both visually and historically; Roebling represents a burgeoning industrial U.S.A. at the turn of the century, with its seventy factory buildings at work day and night. At the same time, Roebling became a typical American melting pot, as its blocks of attached housing provided homes for immigrant workers, its community a base for new Americans.

Roebling's factory was, in fact, a major contributor to the growth of the nation's enterprise and economy. A list of what the Roebling steel plants produced reads like a travelogue of America, for Roebling produced essential steel cables used in building the nation's bridges and skyscrapers.

The Roebling family of three brothers—Washington, the engineering genius; Ferdinand, the financier; and Charles, the planner—already had a plant in nearby Trenton. Their company had created the Brooklyn Bridge with its breathtaking cable design a few years earlier, and they needed more space for their Trenton steel cable company. They chose a tract of farmland—to be called Roebling—just eight miles south of Trenton on the Delaware River and began building in 1905.

They soon realized that their workers would need a place to live. They decided on a "Model Town" that would include 750 brick houses. Charles Roebling, with a love of planning and design, undertook the planning of a new community. He laid out Roebling's wide streets lined with London plane trees; he chose nine different styles of architecture, most in brick with slate roofs. He created a Main Street with shops and a bank, churches, schools, social halls, a recreation center, and a park and open space. The village had an appealing design, with the train depot in the middle of town. A newspaper described Roebling this way at the time: "Not only is every possible want of the employees provided for, but the aesthetic side of the proposition is being worked out to the satisfaction of an extreme idealist."

While the Roeblings believed in creating an idealistic environment for their workers, there were certain conditions that made Roebling as unusual as its esthetic planning. The company owned everything. In order to keep unionization away, the Roeblings imported their workers (never Italians, known for labor agitation) mostly from Eastern Europe. Roebling, with its inexpensive housing and complete village life, was a great draw for immigrants. After arrival, they were housed according to their nationality—one street for Poles, another for Czechs, and so on. Those who knew English were placed farthest from the mill. Though laboring twelve hours a day in the searing heat of a steel plant, these immigrants nonetheless stayed on—many for a lifetime. For many, the comfortable homes with their individual vegetable gardens, the weekly silent movies and band stand concerts, doctors and a hospital, schools, open bars, and congenial neighbors provided a good American life.

At its height the plant produced wire cables used in elevators, construction equipment, piers, stadiums, trams, and material for everything from airports to skyscrapers to refrigerators. During its heyday, Roebling created the steel cables used in many long-span suspension bridges, including the George Washington Bridge, the Golden Gate Bridge, the Manhattan Bridge, the Bear Mountain Bridge, and numerous others throughout the country. Some seventy buildings with about 10,000 people kept busy there in the 1940s.

After World War II, Roebling began its decline; houses were sold to workers, and the company itself was sold and eventually closed, leaving a vast industrial gap of empty buildings. Today, environmental clean-up and tourism are the main activities, as Roebling's citizens commute elsewhere for work.

But a visit here is decidedly interesting, and there is a walking tour to acquaint the tourist with this unusual historic district. (You can easily pick up the tour map at Dolly's Delicatessen on Main Street, or at the library.) If you follow the walking tour map you will begin at the Roebling Inn, on Riverside Avenue near the Delaware riverfront. This was the first permanent building, which served as a boardinghouse for the first workers. Walk from here up 4th or 5th streets to see the brick row houses that typify Roebling. (The larger houses on Riverside Avenue were for company executives.) The General Store on Main Street has been described as one of the nation's first indoor malls—it sold food, clothing, shoes, and pianos, along with practically everything else available in 1906 when it opened. Across the back alley were more stores—a bakery, drugstore, barbershop, and doctor's office. The first schoolhouse was located a block away on Knickerbocker Avenue; a later one was built across the tracks. You'll see the train still come through the center of town. Don't miss the Auditorium and Bandstand. These are just a few of the stops on the tour. The factory complex itself is now only visible through the gates. The village is a step into the past—when paternalistic and idealistic industrialists created a "company town" in the most complete sense.

❧ IN THE VICINITY

In nearby Trenton you'll find **Riverview Cemetery**, where John A. Roebling is buried. His gravestone includes a tribute to his grandson, Washington A. Roebling, who (with his race car) went down with the *Titanic*. Also buried in this most elegantly designed cemetery with many rare trees are Civil War major general George B. McClellan, several industrial titans, including Walter Scott Lenox of china fame, and many early Quakers whose graves have no headstones.

Also in Trenton visit several historic sites of interest:

Old Barracks Museum, on Barrack Street. The only original barracks dating to the French and Indian War, it is also known for its role in Washington's victory over the Hessians. Telephone: 609-633-2709.

William Trent House, at 15 Market Street. Built by Justice William Trent in 1719, the mansion is open to visitors. Telephone: 609-989-3027.

Trenton Battle Monument, at North Broad and North Warren Streets. Here is the site of Washington's artillery for the Battle of Trenton.

39·
RANKOKUS
INDIAN
RESERVATION

Rankokus

An Introduction to
Powhatan Renape Culture

❦ HOW TO GET THERE

From Route 295, take exit 45A. Go east on Rancocas Road for 1.5 miles to exit on your right in the township of Mount Holly.

❦ INFORMATION

The reservation is open on Saturdays from 10 A.M. to 3 P.M. and on Tuesdays and Thursdays by appointment. Guided tours are available, and there are many festival days and other events. Telephone: 609-261-4747; Web site: www.powhatan.org.

❦ The Powhatan Renape Nation is an American Indian nation located here in Burlington County. This reservation functions as both a social service agency for the New Jersey Native American community, and as a center for cultural and historic activities relating to Powhatan and other tribal civilizations. As many as fifty different tribes take part in various events at the reservation. ("Powhatan" refers to the political identity, while "Renape" refers to the ethnic/language identity.)

A visit to this quiet and appealing site is a good way to introduce American Indian traditions and history to children and others with an interest in the Native American past. For here you can hike through particularly lovely wooded trails, see actual buffalo grazing (three of them), visit huts and a traditional woodland village, enjoy a small museum, and watch a variety of Native American events. At several annual festivals a troupe of dancers perform blanket, spear, shield, and friendship dances, give traditional arts demonstrations (including mask making, bow making, and pottery), and American Indian food (such as buffalo and alligator burgers)—all meant to introduce the culture to outsiders and to keep ancient traditions alive. "Wisdom Keepers" share folklore and tribal histories. The annual arts festival is the largest juried Indian arts festival east of New Mexico.

The Rancocas River area of New Jersey and the Delaware Valley was originally home to vast numbers of Powhatans. They hold two of the oldest treaties signed with Europeans; one with England dates to 1646. Powhatans also lived along the eastern seaboard as far south as Virginia, where most made their homes. As their native lands were taken from them by European settlers, their numbers in the East diminished. War, disease, and prejudice led to disintegration and to migrations elsewhere. It was only in the last half century that an effort was made to keep the nation intact as a cultural and political entity.

A census in 1980 found about nine thousand Indians in the state of New Jersey. In 1983 the state gave the Powhatan Renape nation 350 wooded acres here on the banks of the Rancocas River for its own uses. While much of the wooded area was left uncut, the tribe did create grazing fields for horses and buffalo (also used for vast fairs), a small Ancestral Village, the museum, and a variety of theme trails. (There are no living quarters.) At the museum you'll find seventeen dioramas illustrating Powhatan's history and survival techniques. The reservation runs an ambitious program of activities related to tribal culture and its relevance to life today.

A visit here is both peaceful and interesting. Once you leave your car and the long pathway to this unusual site, you hear myriad birdcalls as you pass by small outposts of tribal civilization—a grass hut, a native food trail, and Indian-style design on the side of a building. But unlike some Native American sites we have visited, this one is neither hokey nor obviously set up to entertain. It has a dignified and woodsy ambience, and we were anxious to return to see the festival of Indian dance, the traditional costumes and foods, and even to see the alligator wrestling that was advertised.

40·
MOUNT HOLLY

Burlington County Courthouse

A Walking Tour through a
Village of Colonial Beauty
and Quaker Roots

❧ HOW TO GET THERE

Take exit 5 on the New Jersey Turnpike to Route 541 directly to Mount Holly. As you enter town you will be on High Street; to find Park Drive and the Visitor Center, continue past the center of town to Garden Street; turn right, and go to Park Drive.

❧ INFORMATION

A self-guided walking tour is available at the library (see below) or at the Shinn Curtis Log House Visitor Center. Tours and Open Houses are sometimes offered. Call the library at 609-267-7111 for information, or the Visitor Center at 609-267-9572; Web site: www.mounthollynjtripod.com.

❧ This town was a surprise to us. We are all familiar with the Williamsburg style of colonial towns, where buildings have been moved and restored and residents dress up in colonial clothes and practice colonial arts and crafts for visitors. But how often does one find a town—particularly in busy New Jersey—where the architecture and ambience have been preserved with such a delightful combination of history and bustling present-day activity? Mount Holly is a rare treat. If you are interested in lovely early American town architecture, as well as a place with a significant historical past, be sure to visit here.

Mount Holly welcomes visitors. With a self-guiding map in hand you can find the important historical and architectural sites yourself (or take a prearranged guided tour if you prefer). This is a town that apparently understood that it was a treasure to be saved, long before the recent preservationist movement began in our state. No less than thirty-nine historic buildings can be visited.

Mount Holly was settled in the 1680s by John and Nathaniel Cripps and Edward Gatskill. They chose the site because of its unusual hill (the "Mount" of Mount Holly), which rises 185 feet above the village, and its site on the Rancocas Creek. Originally called Bridgeton because of its many bridges over the creek, the town prospered, with several mills using its waterpower.

Like many other small villages around Burlington, Mount Holly was settled in large part by Quakers, and its history would be tied to Quaker views about independence and abolition. Quakers fleeing persecution in England (and even in the northeastern colonies) arrived in the Burlington area in 1677. When William Penn chose the "middle colonies" as a site for Quaker settlements, the area around Burlington quickly became Quaker country. John Woolman, who would become a leading abolitionist, was a resident of Mount Holly; his *Journal* and "walking journeys" for the cause of abolition of slavery made Mount Holly a noted safe haven on the Underground Railroad (see walk 37).

Mount Holly became a center for patriots well before the Revolutionary War. By the time the Revolution began, the British were widely despised by Mount Holly's people, who were forced to feed and quarter them. When the British turned the Quaker Meetinghouse into a butcher shop and stable, the residents of Mount Holly were more determined than ever to gain independence. (Visit the meetinghouse to see the cuts in the benches made by meat cleavers in this ill-conceived use of the building.) One citizen, John Brainerd, preached independence from his pulpit, and consequently had his church burned by the British. Through acts like these, as well as Quaker attitudes about justice and fairness, Mount Holly became a haven for dissenters and outspoken patriots.

During the war itself—in 1776—a violent skirmish with the British took place. The fierce battle of Iron Works Hill seemed to find the Hessian allies of the British victorious, but the battle was actually a decoy that kept two thousand Hessian soldiers occupied while George Washington was successfully invading nearby Trenton. The Hessians apparently believed they were fighting a much larger force than the small number of Mount Holly patriots who tried to defend their hill. Washington's capture of Trenton at the same time was a notable victory for the Americans.

After the Revolution, Mount Holly took its place as an important New Jersey town; in 1779 it became the temporary capital of New Jersey, and the state legislature met in the town for two sessions in 1779. Its beautiful courthouse (see below) is a testament to its importance in the history of its time.

As slavery became an increasingly volatile subject in the nation, Mount Holly once again played a part in a national debate. Quaker activism on behalf of abolition brought the dissidents of Mount Holly a cause in which they strongly believed. With John Woolman leading the way, the town became a notable stop on the Underground Railroad, like other villages in the Burlington region. A visit to Woolman's house here gives an idea of his importance as a fiery leader of the abolitionist cause. (Several other sites listed below also relate to abolitionism.)

As we undertake the tour of the town, these dramatic and historic trends are clearly evoked by Mount Holly's streetscape and setting. Begin your walk at the Visitor Center on Park Drive, where you can get your self-guided tour map. (The map contains a great deal more detailed information than we are including in the list below.) If the center is not open, go to the library at 307 High Street.

1. The Visitor Center is in a log cabin called the **Shinn-Curtis Log House.** It was built circa 1712 but was not discovered until the 1960s within another house. It is now the headquarters of the Mount Holly Historical Society. Make your way back to High Street, one of the two major streets of historic buildings. Here you will want to see the buildings listed next.

2. **Mount Holly Library**, 307 High Street. This wonderful mansion with marble fireplaces is in the Georgian style and dates to 1830. Be sure to see the inside.

3. **Waln House**, High Street, a red-brick Victorian house with unusual fluted chimneys.

4. **Haines House**, 222 High Street. Dating to 1852, this is a great example of a double house of the Federal period.

5. **Read House and office**, 204 and 200 High Street. Built in 1770 and 1775, these two Colonial buildings belonged to the distinguished resident Joseph Read, a judge and member of the provincial congress.

6. **Ridgway House**, 225 High Street. Circa 1809, this is a Federal-style house.

7. **Slack House**, 211 High Street. Note the herringbone sidewalk and marble steps in front of this Federal-style house.

8. **Burlington County Prison Museum**, 128 High Street. You won't miss this great dark-gray prison and workhouse (the first fireproof building in the country). Designed by Robert Mills, the architect of the Washington Monument, this massive building can be visited Tuesdays through Saturdays.

9. **Burlington County Court House**, 120 High Street. We found this to be the gem of the entire historic town. What a beautiful courthouse this

is! Built in 1796, it is considered to be one of the finest examples of Colonial architecture in the nation. Don't miss it! And note the two small buildings flanking it; these attractive offices were built in 1807.

10. **St. Andrew's Episcopal Church**, 121 High Street, dates to 1844 and is in a Gothic style; it is a Mount Holly landmark.

11. **Friends Meeting House**, corner of High and Garden streets. The date of this colonial meetinghouse is 1775. Be sure to go inside to see the results of the British takeover as a butcher shop in 1778. Visit the adjacent graveyard. Next, turn onto Garden Street.

12. **Isaac Carr House**, 21 Garden Street, is a late-Colonial-style house that was built in 1785. Mr. Carr was one of the owners of the ironworks destroyed by the British during the Revolutionary War.

13. **Chapman House**, 34 Garden Street, was a doctor's residence. It is in the Colonial Renaissance style and was built circa 1775. Next, turn onto Brainerd Street.

14. **Ridgway House**, 10 Brainerd Street. Owned by a bricklayer who built a number of Mount Holly's brick houses, this home was built circa 1760.

15. **Cooper and Dobbins houses**, 12 and 14 Brainerd Street. These two late-Colonial homes were built about 1782. Both have interior chimneys—unusual for the time.

16. **Mann House**, 20 and 22 Brainerd Street. Dating to circa 1785, the building belonged to a Methodist minister.

17. **Thomas House**, 34 Brainerd Street. Built in 1813, it is in the Federal style.

18. **Historic Old Schoolhouse**, 35 Brainerd Street. Don't miss this 1759 school building, the oldest in the state at its original site. It can be visited on Wednesdays from 10 A.M. to 4 P.M., or by appointment. Next, turn onto Buttonwood Street, and walk to Mill Street.

19. **Three Tuns Tavern**, 67 Mill Street. This 1723 tavern building—the oldest in Mount Holly—has a long and interesting history. The British were quartered here in 1776.

20. **Burlington County Trust Company**, 47 Mill Street. This 1815 Federal-style bank building has stained-glass windows and many other elegant architectural details both inside and out. Next, turn onto Pine Street.

21. **Relief Fire Company.** This is the oldest continuously active volunteer fire company in the nation, having been organized in 1752, though this building itself was constructed in 1892. Next, turn back to High Street.

22. **Burlington County Herald,** 17 High Street. This building of 1820 is in the Federal style. Next, turn onto White Street.

23. **Earnest House,** 14 White Street. Built circa 1775, this house is in a typical Colonial style.

24. **Humphries House,** corner of White and Church streets. Built circa 1747, this house is patterned after an English cottage.

25. **Budd House,** 15 White Street. Circa 1744, this Colonial is the earliest known house on its original site in the town of Mount Holly.

These are a few of the most interesting historic buildings, but there are many additional sites not far away, including fine examples of Victorian house architecture. Visit the hill for which Mount Holly is named, and also the John Woolman Memorial at 99 Branch Street.

❧ IN THE VICINITY

Just 2 miles from Mount Holly is **Smithville County Park.** (Take Route 621 east.) This is a most unusual spot. It is not only a green area with a gurgling brook and picturesque ravine, but also a historic site. Here you'll find a grand Greek Revival mansion and a factory and workers' homes that formed the bailiwick of one Hezekiah Bradley Smith, a nineteenth-century inventor and manufacturer. Among his most creative ventures were steam-operated bicycles. Smith converted a failed cotton mill into a bustling complex here, complete with homes, theater, bowling alley, 300 acres of farmland, and other amenities for a planned and complete workers' environment. After Smith died, the company continued and created one of the oddest of New Jersey's many unusual inventions: a bicycle railway to carry workers from Mount Holly to Smithville. Riders glided on a rail on self-propelled bicycles, at as much as 18 miles per hour. The museum here is open from April through November, Wednesdays and Sundays, or by appointment. Telephone: 609-261-3780.

41 ·
BATSTO

Batsto Village

A Bog Iron Forge Village
in the Pine Barrens

❦ HOW TO GET THERE

From the Garden State Parkway, take exit 52. Turn right onto Greenbush Road to Route 653. This will take you to Route 542 and Batsto's entrance gates.

❦ INFORMATION

Batsto is a New Jersey State Historic Site. The Visitor Center is open from 9 A.M. to 4:30 P.M. daily. The grounds are open from dawn to dusk daily. A fee is charged for parking between Memorial Day and Labor Day. Telephone: 609-561-3262; Web site: www.batstovillage.org.

❦ The Historic Museum Village of Batsto is somewhat of a surprise to visit. It is set in the deeply wooded Wharton State Park of the Pine Barrens, and is thoroughly unlike the various tourist attractions that populate the region at the nearby coastline. The state has done a fine job of retaining and protecting its rustic charm and wide-open spaces and the Mullica River that rushes over the dam that powered the forge. It is a wonderful place to walk, as well as to capture the ambience of a small village of the past. You have to imagine what it must have been like as a hot, smoky, industrial environment a century and a half ago, for today it seems quite idyllic.

First, a word about Wharton State Forest. It is the largest single area of undeveloped land in the state park system (some 110,000 acres). The Pine Barrens are a spectacular, sandy region with pines and blueberries and many rivers and bogs. The Leni-Lenape Indians fished and hunted here even after European colonists built small settlements along the rivers. (Batsto's name derives from the Swedish word for bathing place.) Wharton is named for Joseph Wharton, an industrialist from Philadelphia who owned almost all of the area in the 1870s and planned to dam the streams to provide water for his city. Fortunately, almost the entire area is still as it was when his plan fell through: a vast forest to explore. You might want to combine your visit here with a greater hike on a part of the 52-mile Batona Trail in Wharton State Forest. This is one of the most beloved of the Pine-land's hiking routes, and it can be accessed near Batsto.

Batsto was founded in 1766 by Charles Read of Burlington. It was Read who envisaged a thriving industry developing from the chunks of bog iron that were accessible in the wetlands and creek beds of the area. The red-dish material had been used only for face paint by the Leni-Lenape; Read recognized the deposits and decided to try smelting them at a forge to make iron. (Such bog ore is formed because of the high vegetable content in the water of the Pine Barrens; the deposits are created by the oxidation of these marl beds. As you walk through Batsto, you can see a pile of local bog iron.) Read considered the site ideal: there was plenty of wood for heating the forge, and the swift-moving Mullica River was usable for power and easy transportation.

In 1773 a Philadelphia merchant and ardent patriot named John Cox became the owner of the Batsto Iron Works. By the time the Revolutionary War started, Batsto had become a major arsenal and supplier of iron for the Continental Army, making cannons, ammunition, kettles, pots and pans, wagons, and even ships. (Batsto's iron became so well known that George Washington had his ironwork for his new home at Mount Vernon made at the forge.)

During the war Washington was highly appreciative of Batsto's contributions; he made Cox a colonel and sent a special protective force to guard the village, though the British never attempted to capture Batsto for fear of being waylaid on the Mullica River. A thriving business in privateering helped Batsto become a very profitable site.

The industry changed hands again in 1778, when Joseph Ball bought the property, continuing its thriving business and speculations in captured vessels and cargoes. He became one of the nation's richest men. In 1786 Batsto was again sold, this time to William Richards, whose family continued to own it for a century. It was the Richards family who constructed most of the village buildings we see today. The village was quite self-sufficient, with its own housing, church, village store, sawmill, gristmill, and even salt works. The great ironmaster's mansion that still is the centerpiece of Batsto was constructed by William Richards, who personally oversaw his empire from his hilltop. By 1830 the production of iron had risen to 800 tons a year, and more than three thousand boatloads were shipped out of the village during the next decade.

Batsto's heyday was soon to end, however, as coal was discovered in nearby Pennsylvania, making the bog-iron industry obsolete. Richards added glass production and a paper mill to Batsto's enterprises, but those industries did not manage to sustain Batsto. The Philadelphia industrialist Joseph Wharton purchased the entire village for $14,000 in 1876.

Wharton had a variety of different plans for Batsto, including damming the river and selling the Pineland's pure water to urban areas (a scheme that was denied by the government), raising sugar beets, and growing cranberries. But Batsto never regained its industrial affluence. Wharton nevertheless purchased more and more land surrounding Batsto. His holdings would become Wharton State Park; in 1909 his heirs offered 100,000 acres to the state, as Batsto became a ghost town. It took thirty-nine years before the state purchased the land and began the village's restoration as a historic site.

Today this unusually well kept lakeside village gives the walker a realistic picture of life in a nineteenth-century rural town. You can see and hear the water rushing over the dam as you cross the little bridge in the center of the village; you can visit the interiors (in season) of several of the buildings, including the great mansion; you can hike through the surrounding woods and around the picturesque lake; and you can see an old ore boat used for transporting the bog iron. The oldest house in town is on the south side of the lake. Known as the "Spy House," it was supposedly occupied by a Tory keeping watch on the shipping of munitions during the Revolutionary War. Note the 1852 post office with its thirty-one-star flag, and its portrait of President Millard Fillmore. The ironmaster's mansion, now fully restored, is a sight to behold, fully furnished in various Victorian styles. In season, various crafts are demonstrated in the village shops.

⚜ IN THE VICINITY

Atsion is another iron forge village in the Pinelands. Also important during the Revolution, it converted mountain ore, as well as bog iron. There are several old remains to be seen here, too, but the site is not as extensive as Batsto.

Weymouth also has an iron forge and is an interesting, very remote place to walk, with its ruins and foundations of a mill building along a raceway.

42·
WHEATON VILLAGE

Wheaton Village

A Historic Small Town
with Glassworks

❧ HOW TO GET THERE

Wheaton Village is in Millville in Cumberland County, halfway between Philadelphia and Atlantic City. From the New Jersey Turnpike, take exit 4 to Route 73 north to I-295 south. Go to exit 27 (Route 42 south), then take Route 55 south to exit 26. Follow the brown signs to Wheaton Village.

❧ INFORMATION

Open seven days a week, April through December, from 10 A.M. to 5 P.M. Open Wednesday through Sunday during January, February, and March. Closed on major holidays. Many events are scheduled here; call for information. Telephone: 800-998-4552 or 856-825-6800; Web site: www.wheatonvillage.org.

❧ Wheaton Village is a celebration and historical evocation of one of New Jersey's most important industries of the past: glassmaking. The first successful glassworks in America was opened in this area by Caspar Wistar in 1739. This industry—which produced bottles and windowpanes for the growing population of colonists—was ideal for the area: southern New Jersey had abundant fine-grained silica sand and a vast supply of pine wood for the glassmaking furnaces.

Wistar, a native of Germany, arranged with a sea captain to bring trained glassmakers to America from Germany to teach him the secrets of the craft. In exchange, Wistar provided the craftsmen with homes, food, servants, and a share of the profits. The factory soon began producing everything from windowpanes and utilitarian bottles to elegant glass ornaments. What became known as "Wistarburg glass" had fine, decorated surfaces with whorls of color or white ornamenting the glass. (In fact, some of the techniques for delicate tinting have never been reproduced.) Wistar's success was so widely known that a highway was built to Millville from Philadelphia to bring visitors to watch the process of glassmaking (much as we can do today at Wheaton Village). Today Wistarburg glass is a collector's item.

Before long, Wistar was joined by numerous other glassmakers who opened their own factories. Although Wistar's factory closed under the watch of his son in 1781, by the late 1800s some seventy other glassworks were functioning in Millville, Bridgeton, and the surrounding area. Numerous waterways allowed for easy transportation of their wares. And by 1854 a railroad was running from the coast to Camden. Not all the glass-works were successful, however. After the Civil War a number of them failed—you can still see the remains of one such enterprise in two ghost towns called Hermann City and Bulltown on the Mullica River. We are fortunate that Wheaton Village has been preserved so that we can get a good idea of what life was like in the many small glass making villages of the region.

In 1888 Theodore C. Wheaton, a physician and pharmacist, bought a glassworks in Millville. As a pharmacist he realized the growing need for glass containers, and today Wheaton Village gives us an idea of what the T. C. Wheaton Company and its accompanying village were like a century and more ago. In addition to the factory, there was a full village, with shops, a schoolhouse, homes, and a general store.

Today you can visit the working replica of the factory, where you can watch hot molten glass become a delicate object—and create a small glass object yourself. In addition you can enjoy a variety of craft shops, ride in a half-scale railroad, and even watch a medicine show. Of major interest is the Museum of American Glass, containing some seven thousand glass items. Wheaton's bustling craft center now includes a variety of shops and demonstrations. The most interesting, of course, is watching glass artisans at work, shaping, blowing, and molding the hot glass with nineteenth-century techniques. But you need not only be an observer; some of the many craftspersons allow you to participate. The most popular activity among visitors is making paperweights.

However, this village is not only interesting as a craft center and re-creation of a major New Jersey industry of a century ago. Wheaton Village will also remind us of the way of life in a mid-nineteenth-century rural village, with its one industry, its self-sufficient main street amid surrounding natural beauty. It is the layout of the village, with its long central roadway bordered by great trees, a lake, a traditional village green, and charming small buildings that truly evokes a bygone era.

Carl Sandburg celebrated Millville's glass furnaces in his work "Millville," in which he wrote: "Down in Southern New Jersey, they make glass. By day and by night, the fires burn on in Millville and bid the sand let in the light." Today Wheaton Industries, still a family-owned company, is one of the top glass manufacturers in the world. But their factories have moved into Millville itself, and this romantic small town is a reminder of the growth of American industry from its rustic beginnings to international prominence.

❀ IN THE VICINITY

A historic house called **The Mansion House** is in the nearby town of Millville. It was built in 1804 by David C. Wood, the owner of an iron foundry, and is a nice example of its period.

43·
RED BANK
BATTLEFIELD

Whitall House, Red Bank

*A Picturesque
Riverside Historic Site
and Walking Trail*

❧ HOW TO GET THERE

From Route 295, take exit 24A (if you're heading south) or exit 23 if heading north at the town of National Park. Go through the town to its western edge, on the banks of the Delaware River. The battlefield is at 100 Hessian Avenue.

❧ INFORMATION

The battlefield is open from dawn to dusk daily. The park includes the historic Whithall House where wounded soldiers were tended; it is open on weekends through the summer from 1 to 4 P.M. or by appointment. A map of the battlefield is available at the Park Ranger's Office near the parking lot. Telephone: 856-853-5120 or 856-468-0100; Web site: www.co.gloucesternj.us/parks.

❧ Red Bank Battlefield (not to be confused with the town of Red Bank near the Jersey shore, by the way) is a beautifully situated National Park site on the banks of the wide Delaware River. It is a lovely, 44-acre green expanse overlooking the water and would be a particularly pleasant site for a walk even without its interesting history. Its very setting on the heights near the mouth of the Delaware opposite the Philadelphia side of the river explains its historic past. The panoramic park—now outfitted with picnic pavilions and playgrounds for the pleasure of visitors—also contains clear references to its historic past, including the remains of the fort, a Revolutionary War walk, a 1748 house and museum, and many relics and documents.

In the fall of 1777 the British were in dire need of food and supplies in Philadelphia. Their ships were moored at Chester at the mouth of the Delaware, but American forces controlled the water route from forts along the river. As supplies of ammunition and food diminished in Philadelphia, British troops were put on half-rations. They needed to open up the river.

The Americans submerged several barriers of iron-pointed timbers across the river, blocking large ships from sailing to the city. These barriers were known as *cheveux-de-frises*. The largest and most effective such barrier was at Fort Mercer at Red Bank. Although the fort had not been completed, it was ready for the attack the Americans expected. Colonel Christopher Greene, the American in charge, refused to surrender in advance, and on October 22, 1777, a force of some two thousand Hessian soldiers, who were fighting with the British, attacked Fort Mercer on the heights at Red Bank. Only four hundred Americans from Rhode Island defended the fort and its river barrier.

But Colonel Greene had erected a dummy wall and a small pentagonal "redoubt" in the center of the fort, and his soldiers fired from its high parapet down on the advancing Hessian troops. In a terrible slaughter, four hundred Hessians as well as their commander, were killed in forty-five minutes—unparalleled losses for the Revolutionary War. The Americans lost fourteen men.

While the land battle was going on, ships on the Delaware joined in the firefight. Here too the British sustained heavy losses, with one sixty-four-gun battleship running aground and burning up, and another eighteen-gun ship destroyed.

The victory at Red Bank was a great reverse for the British. But they didn't give up. Continuing nighttime bombardment of Fort Mercer, they eventually caused the Americans to retreat. Greene and his men, not knowing reinforcements were on the way, abandoned the fort and slipped across the river to Pennsylvania, but before they left they burned the fort and everything around it to the ground.

Despite the loss of the fort, the Battle of Red Bank had a significant impact on the war. It is suggested by some historians that the French would not have entered the war on the American side without the victory at Red Bank, or the victory at Saratoga that same week.

At Red Bank today you'll see the James and Ann Whithall House, which the Quaker couple turned into a hospital to tend the wounded. Inside the house today are all sorts of relics and mementos of the battle, including cannonballs, and examples of the great boxes of spikes that were chained to the river to puncture the hulls of enemy ships.

If you choose to follow a particular walk through the park, there is a one-mile loop that begins at the parking lot and proceeds to the major sites of interest: the fort's remains, the place where the *cheveux-de-frises* were attached, the Whithall House, and the tall monument erected in 1905 to commemorate the battle. Although certainly not as grand in size as many other preserved battlefields in the state, Red Bank, with its wonderful setting, is an evocative historical reminder of the ingenuity of the Colonial Army.

❧ IN THE VICINITY

C. A. Nothgale Log House, in Gibbstown at 406 Swedesboro Road, is America's (and in fact the Western Hemisphere's) oldest surviving log cabin, built by Swedish-Finnish settlers in the mid-1600s. Telephone: 856-432-0916.

Old Sweden Trinity Episcopal Church, in Swedesboro, is a 1784 building with two historic cemeteries.

44·
FORT MOTT,
PEA PATCH ISLAND,
AND THE FINN'S POINT
NATIONAL CEMETERY

Fort Mott

*Coastal Ramparts,
Towers, a Ferryboat Ride,
and Civil War Memories*

❧ HOW TO GET THERE

Take exit 1 on the New Jersey Turnpike and Route 49 east for about 4 miles, following signs to Fort Mott State Park. It is located at 454 Fort Mott Road, Pennsville.

❧ INFORMATION

Fort Mott State Park is open daily, from 8 A.M. to 8 P.M. in summer and September weekends, 8 A.M. to 6 P.M. in spring and fall, and 8 A.M. to 4 P.M. in winter. To climb a tower, you must visit from noon to 4 P.M. on the third Sunday of the months between April and October. A self-guided walking tour map is available at the site, and there are also guided tours. Telephone for ferry schedule and other information: 856-935-3218; for Pea Patch Island: 302-834-7491; Web site: wwwstate.nj.us/dep/parksandforests/parks/fortmott.html.

❧ This is a surprisingly fascinating place for a history walk. There are several intriguing aspects of a visit here. Walkers couldn't ask for a more picturesque, open, and inviting place for a hike and a picnic (including a special trail through the marshes on the banks of the Delaware River). For military and architectural buffs, the huge fortifications still extant here are extraordinary, and you can walk all over and through them. And a visit to the remains of the island Civil War prison camp and the Confederate graveyard set among the marshes is undoubtedly one of the most evocative and touching experiences you could imagine. Don't miss this outing.

The first fort at the site of Fort Mott was built in 1643 by the Finns and Swedes whose settlement here was one of the first in the area. Its aim was to control Dutch shipping along the Delaware River, but only ten years later it was abandoned.

It was not until the 1830s that the United States government proposed a fortification for the site, as part of a three-fort plan to protect the Delaware River and its major shipping and industrial interests, as well as Philadelphia, just upriver from here. By the Civil War, it had become part of a military buildup all along the coast.

What we see today, however—the great hulking ramparts and complex stairways and fortifications—slowly took shape after 1872. But it was not until the threat of the Spanish-American War that work was undertaken with a sense of urgency. Big guns were brought in and concrete barriers constructed. The fascinating complex we see today was completed in

1897, but no shots were ever fired from Fort Mott. By World War I the fort was already considered obsolete, and it was closed in 1922.

For those visitors with a taste for military history and armaments, Fort Mott is in fact a most interesting site, with its underground passageways, its bulkheads, and complex architecture. With its many stairways and labyrinth-like corridors, children will love this outing. (The large, dark underground spaces were actually used by mushroom farmers after decommission) Thus, Fort Mott is a sort of military-historic site without a war—or even one battle—of its own, but it serves as a splendid and stimulating place to explore.

Its spectacular remains consist of a coastal defense system: a 750-foot-long, 35-foot-thick concrete and earthen embankment, a sort of parapet wall that rises above the marshy land and water just beyond. Behind the embankment are a complex series of gun emplacements, powder and shell magazines, ammunition hoists, storage areas, and a great number of open-to-air staircases. You can wander around, atop, within, and back and forth throughout this extraordinary site. The views are great and there are also trails and paths and lookouts wherever you venture. For a more detailed description of the fortifications, see the tour material offered at the site.

Two steel range-finder towers, built with unusual, visible, metal skeleton structures, can be climbed for a great view of the surrounding water and vistas. Originally planned to direct gunfire at harbor targets, they are now relics of the past. One tower is at the northern end of the fort and the other sits on the grassy area opposite the park office.

Three Forts Ferry will take you from Fort Mott to Fort Delaware (administered by the state of Delaware) on Pea Patch Island nearby. Here an infamous Confederate prison camp existed during the Civil War. Notorious for its inhumane conditions, Pea Patch Island had 12,500 prisoners by 1862. They were interred in the swampy setting (three feet below water level) without fresh drinking water or the most rudimentary necessities. Many had been captured at the Battle of Gettysburg. Sometimes compared to the infamous Andersonville Prison in the South, Pea Patch Island became so disease-ridden that some 2,700 inmates died there. When space ran out at Pea Patch Island, the cemetery at Fort Mott was used for burials.

A visit here includes an old granite, pentagon-shaped fort (1849), a 40-foot moat with drawbridge, parade grounds, sundry cannonballs, and several buildings that reportedly took 25 million bricks to complete. Today in ruins, the complex's horrible history seems very distant indeed.

Back on the New Jersey coastline, you can either walk on a lovely trail through the scrubby marshland or drive a few minutes to reach the Finn's Point National Cemetery (follow signs). This is a rarity for New Jersey: a Confederate shrine. Buried here are the remains of 2,436 Confederate soldiers, many captured at the Battle of Gettysburg and brought to the dreadful camp on Pea Patch Island nearby. It was not until 1875 that the terrible story of the camp became known, when Southern families still had no news of their sons lost a decade before. After a strong letter from the governor of Virginia, the U.S. Department of the Army made Finn's Point into a National Cemetery, and today it remains a sad symbol of Civil War carnage.

We have visited many graveyards of historic interest in the state, but none captured the great evocation of war quite like this one. Instead of elaborate tombs for important people, here only a few small white stones set within four acres surrounded by a gray stone wall represent these thousands of lost soldiers. An 85-foot-high monument lists their names and home states—from all over the Confederacy—and there are scraps of verse here and there. (The solemn words of Theodore O'Hara's "The Bivouac of the Dead" seem thoroughly appropriate.) The tall, wild reeds—in contrast to the well-kept green lawns of the graveyard—wave in the wind outside the stone wall. The cemetery also has a monument to the memory of the 105 Union soldiers, a few veterans of the Spanish American War and World War I, and the graves of thirteen German prisoners of World War II. The absolute silence (except for birdcalls) of this small memorial makes it a suitably somber and beautiful site.

❧ IN THE VICINITY

Finn's Point Rear Range Light. (Take Fort Mott and Lighthouse Roads from Fort Mott.) This is a 115-foot-tall wrought-iron lighthouse dating to 1876. Originally designed to help sailors navigate the difficult Delaware River channel, it has a 119-step spiral staircase and is an unusual-looking lighthouse, recently preserved and placed on the National Register of Historic Places.

45·
GREENWICH

Greenwich Tea Burners' Monument

*The Unspoiled Site of New Jersey's
Own Revolutionary "Tea Party"*

❧ HOW TO GET THERE

From exit 1 on the New Jersey Turnpike, take Route 49 east as far as Shiloh. Take Route 620 (the Greenwich-Shiloh Road) south to Route 623 into Greenwich.

❧ INFORMATION

The Cumberland County Historical Society will arrange tours, or give you a self-guided walking tour map. They also operate a museum in town that is open from April through November, Tuesday through Saturday from noon to 4 P.M., and Sunday from 2 to 5 P.M. It is located in one of the historic buildings, the Gibbon House (see below). Once a year, historic houses are open to visitors; call for the date. Telephone: 856-451-8454; Web site: www.cchistsoc.org.

❧ Greenwich is one of those unspoiled towns that is both a picturesque place for a walk and a site of genuine historic interest. The village, with some forty eighteenth- and nineteenth-century places to see, is listed in the National Register of Historic Places. Its leafy green setting on the banks of the Cohansey River makes it a particularly attractive spot to visit, though there is no real downtown or town green. This is a thoroughly uncommercial place, and just right for a history walk.

A Quaker refugee from England named John Fenwick founded the village in 1675 (seven years before Philadelphia). It was Fenwick's second settlement; he had already established Salem nearby. He designed Greenwich as a straight, two-mile stretch (from the river toward Salem) of an unusually wide thoroughfare lined by fine manor houses on 16-acre plots. Though he did not live to see Greenwich's settlement completed, his plan was followed by his fellow Quakers, including William Penn. A map drawn in colonial times (and available at the Historical Society) gives a good idea of the long, straight Ye Greate Street of Greenwich's colonial past that is still today a pleasant, spacious avenue.

Fenwick and his Quaker brethren were firm believers in religious tolerance. From its earliest days Greenwich welcomed a variety of churches, several of which are still extant. It also provided one of the first schools for the poor; the building still stands.

By 1695 Greenwich was a thriving shipping port for foreign goods. The river was filled with sailing ships and laden barges—and a number of smuggling enterprises. In 1701 the village became an official port of entry for West Jersey, and Market Square was designated the site for annual fairs by the royal governor.

But improving roads, and the choice of nearby Bridgeton in 1748 as county seat, dealt Greenwich economic blows, and its shipping industry diminished, preserving for us today its wonderful, unspoiled charm. By the mid-eighteenth century, Greenwich was becoming increasingly angry with the tariffs and impositions of the British, and Revolutionary fervor was growing.

In 1767 the Townshend Acts put a heavy tax on tea, as well as other necessities. Townshend, knowing how American women adored tea, assumed the tax would be ignored. But Americans were infuriated; instead of paying the tea tax they turned to smuggled Dutch tea, boycotting British tea. The men of what became known as "Smuggler's Woods" were among the first troops in what would become part of the battle against "taxation without representation." And by 1774 Greenwich would take its place in Revolutionary War history.

The event that was to put Greenwich in the history books was not unlike the Boston Tea Party—but is far less widely known. On December 12, 1774, a brig called *The Greyhound* arrived from England, carrying the offending taxable tea from the East India Company despite the colonists' boycott of British tea. The captain, fearing for the safety of his cargo in Philadelphia, decided to unload at Greenwich instead. A loyalist merchant named Daniel Bowen offered him a basement in which to store the tea, so that it could be smuggled overland into Philadelphia on another day.

But the news leaked out, the unloading was witnessed by villagers, and soon it was widely known throughout Cumberland County. Ten days later, on December 22, Greenwich had its own "Tea Party." A group of local men from Greenwich and the surrounding area dressed up as Indians with war paint (but nonetheless recognizable to their neighbors) and broke into Bowen's cellar storage area in the middle of the night. They stole all the tea and made a great bonfire of it in the center of the town. Villagers cheered them on. Among the tea burners were leading citizens of Greenwich.

At a trial for arson a few months later, seven Greenwich citizens were acquitted by a jury of their friends and fellow patriots; the defendants were also closely related to both the sheriff and some of the jury. Three of the tea burners went on to become outstanding members of the new American government after the war, including two future governors of New Jersey, Richard Howell and Joseph Bloomfield.

A walk in Greenwich is like a visit to a corner of greenest England. You might begin your exploring along the 100-foot-wide, tree-lined Greate Street at its beginning, where Route 620 meets Route 623. That will give you quite a long walk to its end at the Cohansey River; you can also park at the intersection of Bacon's Neck Road and Greate Street to include many of the historic buildings in a somewhat shorter route. Opposite the corner of Bacon's Neck Road you'll find the lovely 1728 Stone Tavern, the oldest tavern in the country (now privately owned) whose sign once read "Bed and Board for Man and Beast." Nearby is the fine Gibbon House, now the headquarters of the local Cumberland County Historical Society. This 1730 home is worth visiting for its beautifully furnished rooms, its Colonial-style kitchen, and its three bricked-up windows on the second floor (a way to avoid the glass tax imposed by the British). While at Gibbon House, pick up a map of the many sites you want to see, and visit the tiny Swedish log cabin in the back garden. It dates to 1650 and was used as a granary. (It was moved to this site.)

Among the sites along Greate Street are a number of interesting buildings, including a 1770s Quaker Meeting House and graveyard, the 1810 school building, the 1852 Presbyterian Church, a Maritime Museum, the Richard Wood House and Store (thought to be the oldest standing in the country), and many others. About one block after Gibbon House, and across Greate Street you'll find the monument to the Tea Party. It was unveiled in 1908 and is still standing at Market Square.

If you want to see the harbor, take Bacon's Neck Road to Tindall Island Road and head toward the water. Today there is a restaurant and boat-building dock at the water's edge, but seeing the surrounding coastline, it is easy to envisage the smuggling that went on in this still very rural and isolated spot.

❧ IN THE VICINITY

Alliance Burial Ground. If very old graveyards interest you, this is a must. About half a mile north of the historic district, you'll find the graveyard across the street from the nineteenth-century church (its predecessor burned down in 1739). Here, in an iron-gated setting, are over one hundred graves, including those of seven of the participants in the Tea Party, as well as many other patriots.

Salem. The nearby town of Salem is worth a stop. It was also an early Quaker settlement and is noted particularly for its distinctive patterned brickwork buildings. There are a number of early buildings on Market Street. The Alexander Grant House at 79–83 Market Street is home to the Salem County Historical Society; you can get a map and listings of historical sites there. Several sites—including the lovely Presbyterian Church—are within walking distance. Telephone: 856-935-5004.

Hancock House. South of Salem (take Hancocks Bridge Road), you'll find Hancock House, a fine brick home built in 1734 by a Quaker, Judge William Hancock. The exterior of the house is another excellent example of the pattern and colored brickwork favored by colonial settlers in the Salem region. Patterns include blue and red zigzags and checkerboards. The house is open Wednesday through Sunday, year-round.

46·
BRIDGETON

Bridgeton

*Exploring a
Cumberland County
City's Historic Legacy*

❀ HOW TO GET THERE

From the New Jersey Turnpike, take exit 1 to Route 49 through to Bridgeton.

❀ INFORMATION

Bridgeton is well equipped for visitors, though it is rarely crowded. The Information Center is located in a former railroad station at the corner of West Broad and North Pearl Streets (Routes 49 and 77). Walking tours, trolley tours, and self-guided maps are available. Telephone: 800-319-3379; Web site: www.historicbridgeton.com.

❀ This Cumberland County town has a long history—from Leni-Lenape settlement to bustling nineteenth-century industry, to today's odd mix of eras and neighborhoods. A visit here can combine a taste of Indian life, Swedish settlement, and historic district Victorian homes—some 2200 land-marked buildings (the largest such district in the state)—many dating to the nineteenth century prosperity of the manufacturing center. Bridgeton's site along the Cohansey River (a major outlet to Delaware Bay) gave the town both its waterpower and easy transportation to nearby cities. Now over 305 years old, Bridgeton is a mixture of wonderful historic sites, nondescript urban sprawl, and large areas of fine Victorian homes. It is quite a large town, and not the easiest to navigate, and we suggest you use your car for the longer distances involved, and then get out and walk.

Leni-Lenape Indians were living in the area in 1686 when the first European settlers arrived. The George Woodruff Indian Museum (see below) has amassed some 20,000 artifacts gathered in the immediate area, including clay pots and pipes and implements. An understanding of Bridgeton's history will necessarily start here. The Tribal Headquarters at 18 Commerce Street is another Native American site, with a library and genealogical records.

In the late seventeenth century, the first European settlers arrived. In 1686 a sawmill was built by Richard Hancock on this spot on the Cohansey River; his was the first of many enterprises to use the waterpower of the river. Soon settlers from Sweden began arriving. The New Sweden Farmstead Museum (see below) is a faithful, handmade re-creation of a Swedish farmhouse and surrounding buildings, including barns, stable, and smokehouse. It is one of the only major testaments to the vibrant Swedish community that settled in southern New Jersey.

Bustling Bridgeton became a center of patriotic activity in the second half of the eighteenth century. During the Revolutionary War, Potter's Tavern (see below) was the center of the town's revolutionary fervor. On Christmas Day in 1775, an issue of a broadsheet called *The Plain Dealer*, protesting Britain's rule, was posted on its door. New Jersey's own Liberty Bell is in the Cumberland County Courthouse in Bridgeton; it tolled on July 4, 1776. Potter's Tavern has been restored and is now a museum.

In 1814 a raceway was dug to make the river more useful to manufacturing, and the major industry, the Cumberland Nail and Iron Company, became the most important Bridgeton industry. It is memorialized in the unusual Nail Mill Museum (see below), which is housed in the original 1814 office of the company. On your visit, be sure to note the odd two-faced clock located in the museum. A grandfather clock, made in 1830, it is attached to the wall in the office, but one face can be seen by outdoor passers-by. The nail company had buildings on both sides of the river, connected by a footbridge. Workers carried materials (including the sheets of iron produced by the factory) over the river to the nail-making machines on the opposite bank.

Other industries provided a good living, too, and more and more fine homes were constructed in town during the nineteenth century. These range from elegant Colonial and Federal homes to the many magnificent Victorians lining the streets. Architectural styles abound in the historic district's large, leafy, and very walkable neighborhood. One of the fliers you can pick up at the Information Center describes and pictures twenty different styles of houses one can see in Bridgeton.

In 1903 the town purchased the huge swath of land that became the Bridgeton City Park and a center for several of the museums. Today it is an excellent place for hiking and biking, as well as visiting the various historic sites it encompasses. In the twentieth century, the heyday of Bridgeton's prosperity was well past and the town slipped into obscurity. It is only in the last decades that a revitalized tourist industry has developed after Bridgeton's placement on the National Record of Historic Places. Today there are all kinds of events, with many of them taking place on the newly created riverfront.

Your outing will necessarily be in three parts. The **George Woodruff Indian Museum** is located at 150 East Commerce Street. Stop here for a terrific overview of Native American life in Cumberland County three centuries ago. Telephone: 856-451-2620.

We suggest you drive to your next site, the **Bridgeton City Park.** Within it you'll find the **New Sweden Farmstead Museum** on Mayor Aitken Drive (telephone: 856-455-9785), and the **Nail Mill Museum,** also on Mayor Aitken Drive (telephone 856-455-4100). You can park at either museum and walk around the grounds. At the New Sweden Farmstead you'll enjoy the log cabin atmosphere and be amazed by the incredibly small buildings these early settlers inhabited. This re-created farm offers a delightfully rustic view of what it was like to live in a farm setting in America's early days. At the Nail Mill Museum nearby, you will get a feel for the Industrial Revolution in America through artifacts and displays. (Think of the importance of nails to new settlements!)

The third part of your walk will begin at the junction of Commerce Street and Mayor Aitken Drive, as you exit the park. Take Commerce Street west to see the houses along Giles Street and Lake Street, where many of the finest houses can be seen. From Lake Street take Franklin Drive. Here you'll enjoy the home of the nail mill's owner: David Reeves lived in the 1850 Italianate house off Franklin, above the mill. From here, go to 51 West Broad to see Potter's Tavern (telephone: 856-455-4055).

Also on Broad, on the corner of West Avenue, is the Old Broad Street Presbyterian Church. It has never had electricity and all events are still held by candlelight. The interior is heated by two original Atsion cast-iron stoves. It is open only rarely. Telephone: 856-455-0809.

These are only the highlights of this very vast and interesting city. Your maps and guides from the Information Center can identify what is of most interest to you and give you maps for the appropriate walking tours.

✿ IN THE VICINITY

Alliance. Take Route 540 to Norma and turn left on Gershel Avenue, which will take you to the remains of a tiny nineteenth-century Jewish settlement at Brotmanville. The Alliance Cemetery, a tiny synagogue, and a small brick chapel containing relics and documents recall the farm settlement in the 1880s here. It was one of some one hundred such Jewish communities farmed by newly arrived immigrants who preferred life in the countryside to city tenements. Alliance was founded near Vineland in 1882 and was eventually home to five hundred people. By the 1920s most had moved away.

47·
EAST POINT
LIGHTHOUSE
TO MAURICETOWN

East Point Lighthouse

The Oyster Boat Route

❧ HOW TO GET THERE

From the Garden State Parkway take exit 17 to Route 9 south. Go west on Route 83 to intersection with Route 47 north. Take Glade Road to your left (just after Moore's Beach Road). Follow signs to Lighthouse Road and East Point Lighthouse in the town of Heislerville.

To Mauricetown from East Point Lighthouse, return on East Point Road and go left on County Road 616 (Heislerville-Leesburg Road) along the river. You will pass through Leesburg and Dorchester. At Route 47, go left. When you reach Route 670 make another left to enter Mauricetown.

❧ INFORMATION

The grounds of the East Point Lighthouse are open all the time, but you should telephone ahead for hours of operation. Group tours may be arranged. Telephone: 856-785-1120; Web site: www.co.cumberland.nj.us/tourism/lighthouses/#5.

❧   East Point Lighthouse is probably as remote a coastal spot as you will find in our populous state. A visit here is strangely silent—except for the songs of seabirds (including gulls and herons) and the whistle of the wind through the high reeds and tidal marshes that surround it. History buffs and nature lovers, as well as beachcombers, will relish this unusual spot.

East Point Light is the second oldest lighthouse in New Jersey (after Sandy Hook). It is a pretty, whitewashed brick structure in a Cape Cod style, with a small tower atop it, and it sits all alone on a bluff above Delaware Bay at its intersection with the Maurice River. The lighthouse was constructed in 1849 to guide oyster boats and other vessels into the mouth of the Maurice River.

Throughout the nineteenth century, sea captains sailed their three-masted schooners and oyster boats through the Delaware Bay and up the Maurice to Mauricetown and Greenwich. (See walk 45.) Oysters became a major industry in the bay and shipping lanes were very busy. Lighthouses were essential along the shoreline, and East Point Lighthouse, which began using kerosene for its light in 1860, was positioned at a major route. Once part of a network of lighthouses along Delaware Bay, East Point Lighthouse is now the only one left.

At the end of World War II, as commerce ebbed in the small villages near Delaware Bay, and as the oyster crop diminished, the lighthouse was decommissioned. It became a lost and much vandalized site until it was reinstalled in 1980 and recently restored by volunteers from the local historical societies. If you make an appointment you can visit the historic interior of the building.

You can walk in and around this antique building, and down to the beach below the tidal marsh that surrounds it. In April and May take note of the millions of horseshoe crabs that make their way to the sandy beach below the lighthouse to lay their eggs. At approximately the same time, shorebird migrations occur in the skies above this scene. It is a bird-watchers' and nature lover's delight.

From East Point drive to Mauricetown, where little seems to have changed since it was the hometown of some eighty sea captains. It is an unusually well preserved town, and with the decline in the oyster industry, has remained quiet and undeveloped. In the nineteenth century, numerous Victorian houses were constructed, along with an attractive 1880 Methodist church, whose spire was occasionally used as a navigational aid. If you enter the church you can climb up to the gallery to see the names of seamen of the past immortalized in stained glass. Mauricetown was built along the winding, picturesque Maurice River, and the town has an old (1888) drawbridge now out of use. The oldest house in town is at the end of South Street—the Caesar Hopkins log cabin of 1650. Hopkins was a Swedish ship captain and one of the earliest European settlers in the neighborhood.

As you walk along these intimate streets with the river nearby, it is not too hard to picture the long-ago arrivals of the graceful sailing ships as they made their way between the guiding light of East Point Lighthouse and the church spire of Mauricetown, bringing them home to their comfortable, close-knit village.

IN THE VICINITY

Bivalve, nearby (from Mauricetown take Route 744 to North Port Norris, and Route 649 to Port Norris and then Bivalve), has a restored oyster schooner on display, and various other mementoes of the oyster trade, which produced one million bushels of oysters a year before a parasite hit the area in the 1950s. Extensive replenishing of oyster beds is now taking place.

48·
CAPE MAY

Cape May

From Colonial to Victorian Pleasures

❧ HOW TO GET THERE

To the town of Cape May: take the Garden State Parkway to its end and follow signs. To Cold Spring Village: take Route 9 from Cape May for three miles.

❧ INFORMATION

Visit these sites in the off-season if you can, as both are crowded in warm weather. Cape May: pick up a map at the Welcome Center (407 Lafayette Street). A map is also available at the head of Washington Street at an information booth. Telephone the Welcome Center for information and events: 609-884-5404; Web site: www.capemaymac.org. Telephone for Cold Spring Village information: 609-898-2300; Web site: www.hesv.org.

❧ Cape May is a Victorian resort that is well known to tourists and vacationers. It is filled with charming homes, historic buildings, horse-drawn vehicles, gaslights, and other accoutrements of the successful resort. In the off-season, you will find it a delight, despite a few too many wreaths on doors, and other twenty-first-century ideas of Victoriana. But don't be put off; the town is actually a treasure trove of true nineteenth-century gingerbread architectural pleasures, and is a great place to walk from street to street to ocean. Not far from the town itself are a number of additional sites of historic interest, so a visit to Cape May will include a variety of experiences, from a colonial graveyard to a reconstructed village to two terrific lighthouses.

It is an interesting fact that Cape May was one of our nation's first resorts—it became a summer getaway before the Revolutionary War. (A newspaper ad in 1766 recommends it.) By 1819, when the first steamship connection from Philadelphia was inaugurated, it was already a fashionable place to vacation. Train service began in 1830. By the 1840s daily ships were arriving. People flocked to the seaside village with its charming streets and beaches. Many stayed in private homes and boardinghouses, but by the mid-nineteenth century great hotels were built, including the 3,000-room Mount Vernon (then the world's largest hotel), which burned down in 1856. (Fires played a continuing role of destruction in Cape May; most of the buildings date to 1878, following another major conflagration.)

Cape May became known as the "playground of presidents," including Abraham Lincoln (still a congressman in 1849), Franklin Pierce in 1855,

James Buchanan in 1858, Ulysses S. Grant in 1873, and Chester A. Arthur in 1893. President Benjamin Harrison used Cape May's Congress Hall Hotel as his summer White House in 1890 and 1891. Other illustrious visitors included Senator Henry Clay (1847) and John Philip Sousa, whose "Congress Hall March" paid tribute to the big hotel. Among the many highlights of a vacation in fashionable Cape May was an auto race early in the nineteenth century between Henry Ford, Louis Chevrolet, and Alexander Christy. (A wave broke over Ford's car, ruining his chances.) Curiously, Cape May owes its architectural preservation to the growth of Atlantic City; the new resort cast Cape May into decline, luring visitors and money to the more northern town. Cape May was left to its Victorian charm and in the last decades has become almost overwhelmed by its own popularity. Numerous events are held here, including Civil War reenactments; telephone the Welcome Center for dates.

Wherever you choose to walk in Cape May you'll find houses and hotels of architectural interest. You can get a self-guided tour map at the Welcome Center, which will point you in the direction of the following notable buildings.

The Cape May Fire Museum, at Franklin Avenue and Washington Street, where you'll see historic fire trucks.

The Chalfonte Hotel, Sewell and Howard Streets, the oldest extant hotel in town, originally built as a private home.

The Emlen Physick House, 1048 Washington Street, a stick-style house designed by the noted architect Frank Furness in 1881. A fine example of Victorian architecture in the center of town, it is also a museum; telephone 609-894-5404 for hours.

The Windward House, 24 Jackson Street, a lovely Edwardian home noted for its stained and beveled glass.

The Abbey, Columbia Avenue and Gurney Street, and 1869 Gothic Revival mansion with stained glass and a 60-foot tower.

Quaker Meeting House, Shore Road. Cape May was first settled by Quakers, and this meetinghouse was built in 1716.

Don't miss the myriad gingerbread houses along practically every street in town.

✿ IN THE VICINITY

Just outside of town are several additional historic sites.

On your map locate the **U.S. Coast Guard Station** where the Continental Navy trained during the Revolutionary War. You can tour it with a self-guided map.

Cape May Lighthouse in Cape May State Park is the third such building to stand on the site; it dates to 1859. The tower is 170 feet high and is located about 100 feet from the shoreline amid the picturesque sand dunes that give Cape May its special aura.

The Hereford Inlet Lighthouse a few miles north of Cape May (111 North Central Avenue in North Wildwood) is often described as "a great Victorian Lighthouse." It was built in 1874 and is the only one of its kind on the East Coast.

Historic Cold Spring Village is an outdoor living-history museum that interprets farm and domestic life of the nineteenth century. It is a particularly good place to take children, as there are twenty-five restored historic buildings and all kinds of crafts, animals, horses and buggies, and a full-costumed cast of characters to bring the past to life. If reconstructed historic sites appeal to you and your family, this is a very complete and interesting one. Among its many enterprises: a blacksmith at work, a leather shop, a jail, a bookbinder, a cobbler, and more. Here too you can get a self-guiding map.

Also in Cold Spring, a very old and very interesting graveyard can be visited. You'll find the **Cold Spring Presbyterian Burial Ground** on Route 162 off Route 9. This 1714 cemetery contains the tombstones of various descendants of the *Mayflower,* some of whom became whalers out of Cape May. There are over a thousand markers in this burial ground, many with still-legible depictions and eighteenth-century inscriptions.

CHOOSING AN OUTING

Place	Walk Number
NATIVE AMERICAN SITES	
Pyramid Mountain	11
Pahaquarra Archeological Site	11
Waterloo Village	15
Rankokus Indian Reservation	39
George Woodruff Indian Museum	46
ARCHEOLOGICAL SITES	
Undercliff	5
Skunk Hollow	6
Long Pond	7
Pahaquarra Archeological Site	11
COLONIAL HISTORY	
Bordentown	35
Burlington	36
Mount Holly	40
Whitall House, Red Bank Battlefield	43
Bridgeton	46
Cape May	48
QUAKER HISTORY	
Bordentown	35
Burlington	36
Mount Holly	40
Salem	45
REVOLUTIONARY WAR	
Jockey Hollow	12
Princeton Battlefield	22
Rockingham State Historic Site	23
Washington Crossing	24
Monmouth Battlefield	25

Place	Walk Number
Red Bank Battlefield	43
Greenwich	45
FORTS AND BATTLEFIELDS	
Jockey Hollow	12
Princeton	22
Monmouth	25
Fort Hancock	27
Red Bank	43
Fort Mercer	43
Fort Mott	44
CIVIL WAR SITES	
Pea Patch Island	44
Finns Point	44
AFRICAN AMERICAN HISTORY	
Skunk Hollow	6
Crosswicks	36
Underground Railroad	37
NATIONAL HISTORIC SITES	
Paterson Falls	1
Ellis Island	3
Ringwood	7
Edison National Historic Site	8
Monmouth Battlefield	25
Georgian Court College	26
Finns Point Rear Range Light	44
HISTORIC CEMETERIES	
Princeton Cemetery	21
Sea Captains' Cemetery	30
River View Cemetery	38
Finns Point National Cemetery	44

Place	Walk Number
Alliance Burial Ground	45
Cold Spring Presbyterian Burial Ground	48

LIGHTHOUSES

Place	Walk Number
Twin Lights of Navesink	27
Barnegat Light	30
Finns Point Rear Range Light	44
East Point Lighthouse	47
Cape May Lighthouse	48

JERSEY SHORE HISTORY

Place	Walk Number
Twin Lights of Navesink	27
Ocean Grove	29
Cattus Island	30
Barnegat Light	30
Cape May	48

PINE BARRENS HISTORY

Place	Walk Number
Double Trouble Village	31
Whitesbog Village	31
Batsto	41

HISTORIC VILLAGES AND GHOST TOWNS

Place	Walk Number
Feltville	9
Speedwell Village	10
Waterloo Village	15
Millbrook	16
Hope	17
Allaire	28
Ocean Grove	29
Double Trouble Village	31
Whitesbog Village	31
Walnford	33
Batsto	41
Wheaton	42

PLANNED AND UTOPIAN COMMUNITIES

Place	Walk Number
Radburn	1
Feltville	9
Roosevelt	34
Roebling	38

HISTORIC MINES AND FORGES

Place	Walk Number
Long Pond Ironworks	7
Speedwell Village	10
Cooper Mill	13
Sussex Branch Rail Trail	14
Sterling Hill Mining Museum	14
Picatinny Arsenal	14
Mount Hope Historic Park	14
Oxford Furnace	18
Batsto	41
Weymouth	41

AGRICULTURAL HISTORY

Place	Walk Number
Fosterfields	10
Howell Living Farm	24
Double Trouble Village	31
Whitesbog Village	31

OLD MILLS AND INDUSTRIAL SITES

Place	Walk Number
Paterson	1
Long Pond	7
Feltville	9
Cooper Mill	13
Clinton	19
Prallsville	20
Walnford	33
Roebling	38
Wheaton	42

HISTORY OF TRANSPORTATION

Place	Walk Number
Whippany Railway Museum	9
Sussex Branch Rail Trail	14
Waterloo Village	15
Delaware and Raritan Canal	23
Lakehurst Naval Air Station	32

Place	Walk Number
OF ARCHITECTURAL INTEREST	
Ringwood	7
Glenmont (Edison's Home)	8
Belvidere	18
Georgian Court College	26
Ocean Grove	29
Bordentown	35
Burlington	36
Mount Holly	40
Cape May	48
VICTORIANA	
Belvidere	18
Ocean Grove	29
Bridgeton	46
Cape May	48
SITES CONNECTED TO NOTABLE AMERICANS	
Alexander Hamilton	2, 3
Early movie stars	4
Cooper Hewitt	7
Thomas Alva Edison	8
General George Washington	12, 23, 24
Albert Einstein	22
Paul Robeson	22

Place	Walk Number
American presidents on vacation	29, 48
HISTORY OF INVENTIONS	
Edison	8
Speedwell Village	10
Twin Lights of Navesink	27
Smithville	40
ARTS HISTORY	
Fort Lee's early movie industry	4
Ringwood's sculpture	7
Georgian Court College's sculpture	26
Bordentown's artist community	35
Wheaton's glassmaking history	42
SETTINGS WITH DEMONSTRATIONS (TAKE THE CHILDREN)	
Fosterfields	10
Battlefield reenactments	12, 22, 25
Cooper Mill	13
Waterloo	15
Walnford	33
Cold Spring Village	48

INDEX

	Walk Number		Walk Number
Acorn Hall	12	Cornwallis, General Charles	22
Air Victory Museum	32	Craig House	25
Alison Park	4	Crosswicks	36
Allaire	28		
Alliance	46	Delaware and Raritan Canal	23
Alliance Burial Ground	45	Dey Mansion	1
Aviation Hall of Fame	32	Double Trouble Village	31
		Drumthwacket	21
Barnegat Light	30		
Barnegat Lighthouse History Museum	30	East Point Lighthouse	47
		Edgewater at Croft Farm	37
Barton, Clara	35	Edison, Thomas Alva	8
Batsto	41	Edison National Historic Site	8
Belvidere	18	Ellis Island	3
Bivalve	47	Einstein, Albert	34
Blackwells Mills	23	Elisha Barcklow House	37
Bonaparte, Joseph	35	Evesham Friends Meeting House	37
Bordentown	35		
Botto House	1	Feltville	9
Bridgeton	46	Finns Point National Cemetery	44
Buccleuch Mansion	23	Finns Point Rear Range Light	44
Burlington	36, 37	Fort Hancock	27
Burr, Aaron	2	Fort Lee Historic Park	4
		Fort Mott	44
C. A. Nothgale Log House	43	Fort Nonsense	12
Cape May	48	Fosterfields Historic Farm	10
Cape May Lighthouse	48	Franklin, Benjamin	36
Cathedral of the Air	32		
Cattus Island	30	Garrett Mountain Reservation	1, 11
Clinton	19	Garretson Farm County Historic Site	1
Clinton, General Sir Henry	25		
Cold Spring Presbyterian Burial Ground	48	George Woodruff Indian Museum	46
Cooper, James Fenimore	36	Georgian Court College	26
Cooper Mill	13	Glenmont (Edison)	8

	Walk Number		Walk Number
Gould, Jay and George	26	Merchants and Drovers Tavern	9
Grant, Ulysses S.	36	Middlebrook Winter Encampment	12
Greene, Colonel Christopher	43	Millville Army Air Field Museum	32
Greenwich	45	Monmouth Battlefield State Park	25
Griffith, D.W.	4	Morristown	12
Hamilton, Alexander	1, 2, 12	Morse, Samuel F. B.	10
Hancocks House	45	Morven Museum and Garden	21
Hermitage	7	Mount Holly	40
Hewitt, Abram	7, 14	Mount Hope Historic Park	14
Hewitt, Cooper	7	Muletenders Barracks Museum	23
Historic Cold Spring Village	48	Museum of Early Trades and Crafts	9
Hope	17		
Hopkinson, Francis	35	Nail Mill Museum	46
Howell Living Farm	24	Naval Air Station Wildwood Aviation Museum	32
Hudson, Henry	27	New Sweden Farmstead Museum	46
Jockey Hollow	12		
		Ocean Grove	28, 29
Kahn, Louis	34	Old Barracks Museum	38
Kastner, Alfred	34	Old Millbrook Village	16
Lafayette, Marquis de	12, 25	Old Millstone Forge Museum	23
Lakehurst Naval Air Station	32	Old Stone House Museum	7
Lambert Castle Museum	1	Old Sweden Trinity Episcopal Church	43
Lawrence, Captain James	36	Old Tennent Church	25
Lawnside	37	Oxford Furnace	18
Lee, General Charles	25		
L'Enfant, Charles	1	Pahaquarra Archeological Site	11
Liberty State Park	3	Paine, Thomas	35
Lindbergh, Charles	1	Palisade cliffs	4
Littell-Lord Farmhouse	9	Paterson Falls	1
Long Pond Ironworks	7	Paterson Museum	1
Macculoch Hall	12	Peapatch Island	44
MacMonnies, Frederick	22	Penn, William	11, 40
Mansion House	42	Perry, Commodore	27
Marconi, Guglielmo	27	Peter Mott House Museum	37
Martí, José	2	Picatinny Arsenal	14
Meadows Foundation	23	Pitcher, Molly	25
Menlo Park	8		

	Walk Number
Prallsville Mills	20
Princeton Battlefield	22
Princeton Cemetery	21
Princeton University	21
Prospertown Schoolhouse	32
Pyramid Mountain	11
Radburn	1
Rankokus Indian Reservation	39
Red Bank Battlefield	43
Red Mill Museum Village	19
Ringwood	7
Riverview Cemetery	38
Rockingham State Historic Site	23
Roebling	38
Roebling, Charles	38
Roosevelt	34
Roosevelt, F. D.	34
Salem	45
Sandburg, Carl	42
Sandy Hook	27
Schuyler-Hamilton House	12
Sea Captains' Cemetery	30
Shahn, Ben and Jonathan	34
Skunk Hollow	6
Smithville County Park	40
Speedwell Village	10
Spermacetti Cove	27
Spring Lake	28

	Walk Number
Sterling Hill Mining Museum	14
Stickley Museum at Craftsman Farms	10
Sussex Branch Rail Trail	14
Tempe Wick Farm	12
Twin Lights of Navesink	27
Undercliff	5
Underground Railroad	37
Van Bunschooten Museum	16
Van Riper–Hopper Museum	1
Von Steuben House	4
Walnford	33
Washington, George	1, 4, 10, 12, 23, 41
Washington Crossing State Park	24
Waterloo Village	11, 15
Weehawken	2
Weymouth	41
Whippany Railroad Museum	9
White, Stanford	7
Whitesbog Village	31
Wheaton Village	42
William Trent House	38
Woodruff House	9
Wortendyke Barn	6
Wright, Patience Lovell	35

PHOTO CREDITS

ABOUT THE AUTHORS

Lucy D. Rosenfeld and Marina Harrison are the authors of eight guidebooks together, including *A Guide to Green New Jersey*. They have published on subjects ranging from history, to gardens and natural sites, to public art. They are life-long friends who love discovering new places to explore. Lucy is the author of more than twenty books on architecture, and Marina has spent many years in social sciences and humanities publishing.